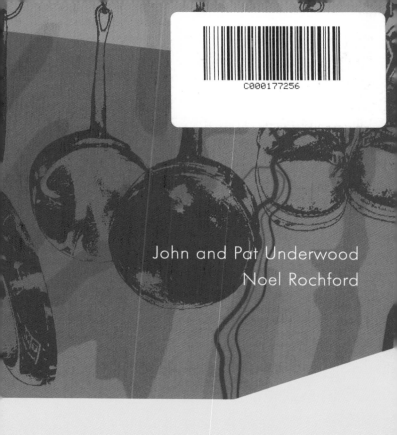

John and Pat Underwood
Noel Rochford

walk & eat
CORSICA

CONTENTS

This pocket guide is designed for visitors to the island who would like to do some fairly easy walking as opposed to tackling the more difficult routes. This may be because it's too hot in high season, or you are travelling with children.

We've hand-picked enough walks, restaurants and recipes to fill a week wherever you are based although, since Corsica is such a large island, not all will be right on your doorstep!

The highlights at a glance:

- 13 varied day walks, each with topographical map
- 1 excursion — on the world-famous 'Trinichellu', Corsica's narrow-gauge railway
- recommended restaurants and hotels
- recipes to make at your self-catering base or back home
- special section with hints on wheat-, gluten- and dairy-free eating and cooking on the island

INTRO

THE WALKS

The walks in this book (a 'baker's dozen') range from easy, flat routes along the coast to fairly gentle hillside hikes. Dotted round the island (see map on page 126), they have been chosen for their *magnificent views or natural surroundings, with the added bonus of a good restaurant nearby.* Special emphasis has also been placed on restaurants that are open outside the peak summer season. For a very wide selecion of island walks, we recommend Noel Rochford's *Landscapes of Corsica,* with over 40 main walks and many variations. It's one of Sunflower's 'Landscapes' guides, a series detailing walks and car tours for some 50 destinations. For more information see www.sunflowerbooks.co.uk.

> Authors' note
>
> As publishers at Sunflower Books, for the last few years we have been updating Noel Rochford's *Landscapes of Corsica* when he has been unable to do so.
>
> Thanks to Noel, we got to know the island many years ago, and he originally devised many of the walks in this book. So the walks are a three-way effort, and the two of us have done the eating and cooking.
>
> — John and Pat

THE RAILWAY EXCURSION

A 'day out' on Corsica's narrow-gauge railway is *not to be missed.* The journey is an excursion in itself — and all the better when combined with a meal at one of the restaurants we recommend — but you can also combine the trip with a short walk.

The train can also be used to reach other walks in the book.

The main line runs between Ajaccio and Bastia, with connections from Calvi and l'Ile-Rousse. The whole trip is rather long, so we have suggested a shorter version depending on where you are based. But many people like to do the entire route; if so, plan to stay overnight at one end.

THE RESTAURANTS

We have *featured* the restaurants (and hotels) we use regularly (or have just discovered) and say why we like them. In each case we include a 'mini-menu' listing some of their specialities. A price guide is given (€ to €€€) to indicate 'very reasonable' to 'fairly pricey'. But remember that you can have a relatively inexpensive meal in a five-star establishment if you just have a light lunch — for instance Corsican soup or the famous omelette with *brocciu*.

No restaurant has paid — in cash or in kind — to be included in this guide.

Some of the restaurants, especially those in the mountains, are at hotels where you might like to spend the night, especially if you want to have dinner there and there is no public transport back to base later in the evening.

THE RECIPES

Most of our recommended restaurants were willing to share with us the main *ingredients* used in their recipes, but the actual preparation remains their 'secret'. We gathered as much information as possible and then cooked all the dishes ourselves, to make sure they 'work' and are at least a fair approximation of the restaurant's version. The recipes selected have been chosen to offer as wide a spectrum of dishes as possible.

What we cannot guarantee, of course, is that they will taste as good back home as they did on Corsica! So many factors come into play to make food taste better when you are on holiday — from the intangibles (the atmosphere and the sense of relaxation after a day's good walking) to

It's very unlikely that you will come face-to-face with any wild boars on the walks in *this* book, but you *will* see them by the roadside, snaffling the chestnuts, mushrooms and nuts that impart such a rich flavour to their meats, whether roasted or smoked.

the tangible (wild boar and *brocciu* are a little hard to come by back home!). So if you are in self-catering, why not try some of these recipes while you're on the island?

We've made all of these dishes on the simple kind of cooker usually found in self-catering (a decent oven is a *must*) — or on a barbecue. And good news for anyone suffering food intolerances: all of the recipes can be **gluten- and dairy-free** (see page 134).

CORSICAN FOOD

Aside from the few times when we've just fancied the local grilled fish, we have always opted for the regional dishes, variously called *menu corse, menu du terroir,* etc.

Assiette régionale at the Auberge de la Restonica — a work of art, with (clockwise from the bottom): coppa (smoked pork fillet), pork terrine and smoked sausage, lonzu (smoked pork shoulder), prizuttu (prosciutto), olives, pickles and chutney

Top of our list would be the **mixed plate of local meats** (see left). (Another meat speciality, not shown, is *figatellu,* a sausage of pork liver and offal usually served fried or grilled on a wood fire; it's on the menu at La Cave in l'Ile Rousse.) **Soups** are a must, from the famous *suppa corsa* (recipe page 102) to fresh soup of Corsican rock fish served with *rouille* (orange-coloured mayonnaise of olive oil, garlic, peppers and saffron).

For a light meal there are omelettes, especially the *omelette au brocciu* (an ewes'-milk cheese similar to ricotta), seasoned with mint (recipe page 25). Other possibilites include endless **pasta** dishes, sometimes with a sauce of fish or seafood, **pizzas** of all descriptions, **mussels** *(moules)* in a variety of sauces — especially at U Furnellu in St-Florent! Another tasty dish is a plate of **fritters** *(beignets)* — usually aubergines or courgettes (recipe page 47) or **stuffed aubergines** (recipe page 24), always served with a tomato sauce.

Down on the coast, the **fish and seafood** is out of this world (if fairly pricey). There is an enormous selection, and the restaurant will usually either grill it, or fry or poach and then sauce it

Corsican wines

Corsica has produced wine since Greek and Roman times; most are strong and full-bodied with a fruity bouquet. We have only had two poor wines — both white and from the southeast. The best wines are produced in Appellation d'Origine Contrôlée areas: Ajaccio, Calvi (Balagne), Côteaux du Cap Corse, Muscat du Cap Corse, Figari, Patrimonio (Nebbiu), Porto-Vecchio and Sartène. All supermarkets stock good Corsican (and French) wines; *Corsican wine is quite pricey.*

Some of our favourites include
white: Patrimonio (Nielluccia, Montenagni, both dry), Muscat de Cap Corse
rosé: Clos Landry (Calvi) and those from Cap Corse, Patrimonio and Porto-Vecchio, also Domaine Vico (from Ponte Leccia)
red: Ajaccio (I Peri), Calvi (Domaine Orsini), Figari (Costa Rossa, Petra Bianca), Patrimonio (Clos de Bernardi and Clos Teddi), Domaine Vico (from Ponte Leccia)
desert wines: many are available — try the fruit or herb flavour that appeals!

in many different ways. While fish is usually *presented* whole (as in the photograph on page 75), it is then removed for filleting if you wish (see page 23). On the other hand, do *not* expect to find a selection of fish dishes up in the mountains … except for the fresh river trout which abounds at places like Vizzavona and Evisa (see recipe on page 57).

While you can get a good steak or veal almost anywhere, more interesting **meats** are to be found in the mountains! Chief among them is **wild boar**, usually served in a stew (*civet de sanglier*). **Veal** is another Corsican speciality, but you may not recognise it! Corsican cattle are raised in the open, not confined to pens. The cuts are thicker and more like pork in colour, and the taste is very different, since the cattle are free-range and graze. **Lamb**, often on the menu as 'milk-fed lamb' *(agneau de lait)* can be a mixed bag in our experience; it certainly did not equate to suckling or baby lamb in any restaurant we visited and was sometimes mutton-like, strongly flavoured but very tender, with quite a lot of fat. **Baby goat** and **suckling pig** also figure on some menus; as well

as **rabbit** and **game** (in the mid-August to December hunting season). Virtually all meats come in a hearty sauce, usually a reduction of red wine, seasoned with herbs of the *maquis* — thyme, rosemary, fennel, sage, majoram, juniper, mint and *nepita* (peppery 'Corsican marjo-ram'). Sometimes olives are added.

Wild boar in chestnut honey sauce with tagliatelli, at Le Comme Chez Soi in Calvi

Pasta is the carbohydrate of choice with most meat dishes and rice with fish, but virtually all restaurants also have potatoes ... and many serve another Corsican speciality, *polenta.* This is sometimes made in the usual way, with corn meal (and may be fried), sometimes with chestnut flour (resulting in a much darker colour).

Corsican **cheeses** are produced from goats' and ewes' milk and vary from fresh (mild and creamy) to really strong matured cheeses. *Brocciu* (from ewes' milk) is the most popular; it is quite like ricotta, and is used in many savoury and sweet recipes. In the shops you'll see a lot of *tomme* cheeses: made from goats' milk, these are not native to Corsica but have become popular in recent years. Fresh figs or fig chutney (recipe page 32) are often served with the cheese course.

We often give **sweet** courses a miss, but less so on Corsica. Almost every restaurant with a regional menu features some version of **chestnut cake**. At La Cave in l'Ile-Rousse, this is 100% chestnut flour; at the Auberge du Col de Bavella they do a chestnut tart (our version on page 41) which they claim is unique on the island. Then there is *fiadone*, a cake made from *brocciu* flavoured with lemon (recipe page 123). But perhaps our favourite of all was the 'Little Napoléon' at St-Florent, for which we give our version on page 89.

And finally: most restaurant portions (especially in the mountains) are *huge.* They didn't mind us sharing a main course, once we told them we wanted to sample as much as possible and could not handle two full 'menus'.

PLANNING YOUR VISIT
When to go
Most people go to Corsica in summer (June to August). Since it can be very hot then (sometimes even 40°C!), we've selected quite easy walks, some with an opportunity to swim, others in shady woods. But if you are not tied to school holidays or overly keen on swimming, then *do* consider going outside the main season; charter flights are available from Easter until early November, and we have specifically recommended restaurants that are open in the 'shoulder' months.

If this book gives you a taste of walking on the island and you want to do more, then without doubt the best walking months are from Easter to May or early June and September and October. You may have to put up with a little rain, but really in high summer it's too hot for strenuous hikes. The rates for accommodation outside July and August are also far more reasonable than in high season.

Where to stay

Corsica is a huge island. If you are not renting a car, it is imperative that you stay as near as possible to the centre of one of the four main tourist bases: **Ajaccio/Porto, Calvi, Bastia** and **Porto-Vecchio**. All of these have a wide range of accommodation, from hotels to villas to camping sites. Ajaccio, Calvi and Bastia are on both rail and bus lines. Porto-Vecchio is only served by bus; there are connections to far-flung places, but you'll have to get up at the crack of dawn. And beware of Porto: bus connections are very limited and the surrounding roads very slow-going.

Even *with* a car, don't expect to see the whole the island on one visit; it will be enough to get to grips with the region around your base and a trip or two into the mountains. And if you are renting a countryside villa, with car, look at a good map before you choose, remembering that you won't average much more than 25-30km/h on any but the major roads.

What to take

Pack simply! You don't have to 'dress', even for dinner, on the island. Instead, concentrate on a (very) few essentials for the walks. While walking boots are recommended for one or two of the walks, they are not essential; just be sure to take some **strong lace-up shoes** with good grip. Carry a **small rucksack,** *always* stocked with a **first-aid kit**, **drinks**, **snacks** and a **mobile phone** (the **emergency** number on Corsica, as throughout the EU, is 112). For shadeless beach/seaside walks, add **sun protection** (hat, glasses, cream, full-length cover-ups) and **bathing things**. For walks in the mountains, add some **warm clothing**, **long trousers**, **spare socks** and — depending on the season, **windproof**, **lightweight rainwear**, **fleece** and **gloves**.

Note: Mineral water is sold almost everywhere in plastic half-litre bottles; *it is imperative that each walker carries at least a half-litre of water — a full litre in hot weather.*

Planning your walks

Wherever possible, we have chosen walks where you have the option of taking **public transport** ... so that you can enjoy a bottle of wine with lunch! Unfortunately this is not always possible on Corsica. If you hire a **car**, and the route is linear, you can sometimes leave your car at the end of the walk and take a bus or train to the start; otherwise the only option is a taxi.

We have **graded our walks** for the deskbound person who nevertheless keeps reasonably fit. Only one of these walks ascends more than 300m/1000ft, most even less. Remember that these are *neat walking times;* it would be wise to *double the time,* to allow for nature-watching and stopping for a meal.

Our walking **maps** are based on the latest IGN 'Top 25' (1:25,000) maps; the number of the relevant sheet is shown at the beginning of each walk, under 'Grade'. Should you wish to go further afield, these maps are available everywhere on Corsica.

Walking safely depends in great part on *knowing what to expect and being properly equipped*. For this reason we urge you to read through the *whole* walk description at your leisure *before* setting out, so that you have a mental picture of each stage of the route and the landmarks. Most of the routes are **signposted** or **waymarked**, and on *most* of these walks you will encounter other people — an advantage if you get into difficulty. Nevertheless, we advise you **never** to walk alone.

ON ARRIVAL
Information
We strongly urge you to call at the nearest tourist office soon after arrival. They can provide you with information about what's on, and *usually* bus and train timetables. Even if you don't think you will be using the train, it's a good idea to stop at a railway station as well and get up-to-date timetables. If you *do* plan to use the train, enquire about special passes (at time of writing there was a 7-day pass with unlimited travel).

Shopping for self-catering
Although you will no doubt want to visit some local markets, farmers and vintners later, make your first port of call the nearest **supermarket**, not only to stock up on essentials, but local specialities as well. The supermarkets on the island are amazingly well stocked with high-quality produce.

Corsican smoked meats (right) and the fish counter (below) at the Casino supermarket in Calvi

All have separate sections for delicatessen items, fishmongers and butchers, as well as bakeries. There are also separate 'kiosks' with regional specialities. Just look at this fish and seafood display at the Casino in Calvi! Most supermarkets open on Sundays; some close for the mid-day break. Aside from staples, you may want to pick up a few extra things that might be missing from your base — like a vegetable peeler or whisk.

Note: *On environmentally-friendly Corsica, plastic carrier bags are* **not** *an option. You buy an inexpensive shopping bag on your first visit and use it for your entire stay — then bring it home!*

<u>Supermarket shopping list reminder</u>

washing-up liquid or dishwasher tablets
paper towels
aluminium foil
soap
tissues/toilet paper
scouring pads
salt & pepper
mineral water
milk/cream*
coffee/tea/ drinking chocolate
butter*

sugar
bread*
juice
wine/beer/cider
olive oil & vinegar
eggs
tomato purée
rice
mayonnaise/ mustard
batteries?
vegetable peeler?
whisk?

*for gluten- and dairy-free alternatives see pages 136-8

Bonifacio, on the southernmost tip of the island, is a must. This dramatically-sited, cliff-hanging town, with its centuries-old narrow streets, is most impressive. Work up an appetite by taking this walk along the windswept cliff-tops, dazzled by the chalk-white limestone bluffs and the sparkling navy blue sea.

bonifacio
WALK

Begin the walk at the church of **St Erasme**, near the western end of the marina-side cafés in **Bonifacio**. (In the Genoese era this was the fishermen's church, since they were forbidden entry into the town.) Climb the flight of steps (**Montée Rastello**) towards the old town. Tall, ancient buildings (with face-lifts) line the steep pedestrian way. The imposing citadel walls rise high above you, on your right. Five minutes up, a magnificent view awaits you at the **Col St Roch**. You look along the sheer curving coast-line of brilliant white cliffs. On clear days you can see the low hills of Sardinia rising in the

Distance: 7.5km/4.7mi; 2h40min

Grade: easy; a walk for all the family. Can be very windy: on such days do *not* venture near the edge of the cliff! *Almost no shade.* IGN map 4255 OT

Equipment: see page 12; stout shoes, bathing things, sun protection and plenty of water recommended

Transport: 🚂 to/from Bonifacio (park by the port). Or 🚌 (see page 132); the bus from Porto-Vecchio is convenient, at least in school term time, but the bus from Ajaccio is *not.*

Refreshments:
plenty of bar-cafés, pizzerias, and restaurants in Bonifacio; *none en route*

Points of Interest:
Bonifacio, with a wealth of historical sites and tourist attractions
cliff formations and coastal flora
old fortifications
Capo Pertusato

southeast. The chapel here at the viewpoint marks the site of the death of the last victim of the Great Plague of 1528, which wiped out 60 per cent of the town's population.

To head out around the cliffs, climb the paved path that ascends to the left ('**Circuit Pedestre des Falaises**'). You have a fine view back towards the strategically-sited town and over into the inlet sheltering the port. Once on the cliffs, hold onto

17

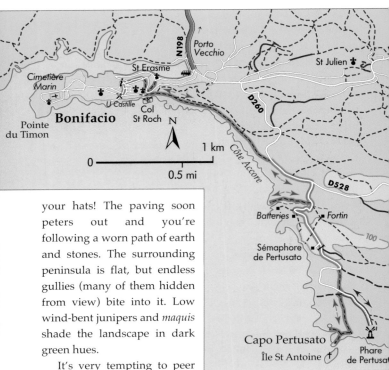

your hats! The paving soon peters out and you're following a worn path of earth and stones. The surrounding peninsula is flat, but endless gullies (many of them hidden from view) bite into it. Low wind-bent junipers and *maquis* shade the landscape in dark green hues.

It's very tempting to peer over the very edge of the cliffs, but *this is exceedingly dangerous*, because there's often a big overhang that could easily crumble away. There are a couple of viewpoints with protective walls; otherwise, keep well back from the edge if it's windy, and supervise children carefully. All

Capo Pertusato: the lighthouse is just visible on the left, behind this monumental salient of rock.

the way along you overlook the wind- and sea-eroded coastline — just magnificent!

You pass the **shell of a building** (**10min**) and fifteen minutes later join the **lighthouse road** (**25min**). Turn right here and, when the road forks (**35min**), head right towards the Phare (lighthouse) de Pertusato. Minutes later you circle a small gully. Strike off right here on a path; it takes you down to the edge of the sea in eight minutes, onto smooth white tongues of limestone.

Take the same path back to the road and ascend past **gun batteries** and, a little further on, the **Sémaphore de Pertusato**. Crossing a crest, you get a closer look at Sardinia, only twelve

At the start of the walk you will see a solitary stack just off the coast. Called the 'Grain du Sable' (Grain of Sand), it is one of Bonifacio's best-known motifs. It would have been part of the limestone cliffs 1000 years ago.

kilometres away. The Iles Lavezzi form the necklace of rocky islets between the two islands; they are part of a protected marine park in the straits. The lighthouse sits alone on the point ahead.

Two or three minutes below the crest, just as the road makes a U-turn, ignore a track going almost straight ahead. But, very quickly after this, take a path off left, ascending through the hillside scrub. Squeezing through the thorny *maquis*, you'll see a wealth of rosemary and red-berried *Lentiscus*. Should you venture upon herds of grazing goats out here, pass them quietly. Five minutes through the scrub you rejoin the road. Turn left and, after 40m/yds, turn hard back to the right on a dirt track. Not far down the track, take the path descending the left-hand wall of a gully that cuts down to the shore. A curious piece of coastline eaten away by wind and water awaits you. A monumental salient of limestone dominates the hilly water-front.

When you reach the water's edge, you discover a small sandy **beach** (**1h20min**), obscured by the rocky shoreline. The small islet of Ile St Antoine, adorned with a cross, hides behind the monumental rock. Climb the rock for another fine view of Bonifacio. A **blowhole** lies unnoticed to the right of the rock. Approach the edge with the utmost care, as it, too, is eaten away underneath. Pay particular attention when gale force winds batter the point here!

You may want to visit the lighthouse (**Phare de Pertusato**), which lies a few minutes along the road to the right (time not included in the main walk).

Otherwise, return the same way to Bonifacio — but note that from the road junction (the 35min-point on the outward walk), you can take a path running just to the left of the road. In calm weather, you can usually follow paths all the way back to the ruin at the 10min-point.

Once back at the **Col St Roch** (**2h40min**), rather than descending the Montée Rastello, take the **Montée St Roch** to the old town ('haute ville'), where you can call at the tourist office, take in the main sights, and have a meal. Then make your way back to the port area.

U Castille

This restaurant straddles both sides of the narrow cobbled alley leading to the famous Escalier du Roi d'Aragon. It has the advantage of being open most of the year, with a small outdoor terrace — a sun trap, even in late autumn. It's fun to sit here and watch tourists

U CASTILLE
Rue Simon Varsi, Haute Ville
(**04 95 73 04 99**
closed Mon and from 15 Dec to 15 Jan €€ **(menu at 23 €)**

entrées include the ubiquitous omelette with *brocciu*, fish soup *(soupe de poissons)*, *moules* or *aubergines à la Bonifacienne* (see overleaf), salad of warm goats' cheese, several pastas — including pasta with salmon or, more unusually, crayfish

fish and seafood of all kinds — squid, swordfish, giant prawns, *pageot* (porgy, a sea bream), red mullet, sea bass, sole, crab

meat dishes: veal, lamb shanks, wild boar stew *(civet de sanglier)*

for a lighter meal and children, there are eight different **pizzas**

The sea bass *(loup)* at U Castille is presented whole, then filleted for you and served with wild mushrooms. Delicious!

making their way up to the steps … and then back down again, having decided it's all too much effort. Or the cars roaring down the alley (little more than a footpath), braking hard opposite the terrace, and picking up their U Castille take-away pizzas. The restaurant has been run by the same family for 15 years, and the service is very friendly.

restaurants

eat

This is *the* recipe for Corsican stuffed aubergines — 'à la Boni-facienne'. Frankly, Pat was a bit disappointed — not with the aubergines, but the *sauce,* which was so strong that it masked the taste of the other ingredients.

A few days later we asked Marie at Le Refuge (page 31) about it. (Marie is full of cooking tips, if she thinks you are really interested in Corsican cooking.) She thought we might prefer the dish made 'à la mode de Porto-Vecchio': the tomato sauce *(without onion)* is simmered for only 5-10 minutes *(not 30min)* and so is less acidic. She also recommends using a *brocciu demi-sec,* not *sec* as in this main recipe. And Pat *does* prefer it Porto-Vecchio-style, but we give the standard recipe here, the one everyone else seems to love!

Stuffed aubergines, Bonifacio-style (aubergines farcies à la Bonifacienne)

Preheat the oven to 180°C/350°F/gas mark 4. Meanwhile, first make the sauce by frying the garlic and onion in a little olive oil until glassy, then combine with the strained tomatoes in a saucepan (fresh tomatoes are used in restaurants, but who has the time!). Add the sugar, salt and pepper and simmer for 30min or more, until it is *very thick.* Set aside.

Cut the aubergines in half, lengthwise, and cook 5min in salted boiling water. Drain and remove the pulp *carefully,* so as not to cut to the skin. Put the pulp in a sieve and drain for 15min, then chop.

Soak the bread in the milk, then crumble it and put in a bowl. Add the 2 garlic cloves, grated cheese, chopped basil, pulp and beaten eggs. Season and mix well. Put the stuffing into a casserole and warm it in the oven for a few minutes, to dry it out, then stuff the aubergines with it.

recipes

eat

Heat about 75 ml of olive oil (5 tbsp) in heavy frying pan and fry the aubergines, *face down*, for 2min, until golden. (This takes some doing, so that the stuffing doesn't fall out — use a couple of long, wide spatulas.) Turn and do the skin side for another 2min.

Put the tomato sauce into a baking dish and place the aubergines on top. Bake for 15min. Spoon some of the sauce on top before serving.

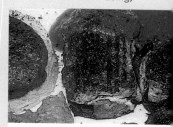

No book with Corsican recipes would be complete without the following dish; it's on all the menus. While we hardly have to tell you how to make a cheese omelette, this one has a twist you might not expect: *you need 8 fresh mint leaves!*

Omelette with *brocciu* (not shown) (*omelette au brocciu*)

For four people, in addition to the mint you will need 300 g *brocciu frais* (or ricotta) and 8 eggs. Break the cheese into largish bits with a fork, and chop the mint. Beat the eggs with a fork and put the cheese and mint in *now*. Season and mix well. Then cook the mixture as you would a normal plain omelette (4-5min one side, 2-3min the other).

Ingredients (for 4 people)
4 aubergines
2 eggs, beaten
150 g stale bread
150 ml milk
100 g *brocciu sec,* grated (or dry ricotta)
a few basil leaves, chopped
2 garlic cloves, crushed

for the sauce
400 g skinned fresh (or tinned plum) tomatoes, juice and seeds removed; strained
1 medium onion, chopped
1 garlic clove, minced
1 tsp sugar
olive oil
salt and pepper

This little-visited walk is one of the most beautiful in the south, and perfect for the whole family. Shady paths, soft with pine needles and aglow with cyclamen in spring, take you to a grassy plateau, from where the *'sportifs'* can forge a way up to the cross on 'Dead Cow Peak'. A superb restaurant will reward your efforts!

forêt de l'ospédale

WALK

2

Start out at the **signpost for the Sentier des Tafoni**, where the Corsican Forestry Department has created a lovely woodland nature trail through the **Forêt de l'Ospédale**. Follow the posts with orange signs showing two balancing rocks *and the yellow flashes,* contouring through the woods. *Ignore* any blue waymarks. You cross two forestry tracks and then meet the orange waymarks of the Mare a Mare Sud heading south from the Col de Mela (**20min**).

The path, bright with wild flowers in spring and early summer, crosses a stream and eventually emerges from the wood at a wide grassy plateau strewn with gnarled pines and 'wild-west' rock formations, the **Foce Alta (40min)**.

Distance: 4km/2.5mi; 1h10min

Grade: very easy ascent of 150m/ 500ft on gentle woodland trails. Additional, *adventurous* ascent of 150m to the top of Punta di a Vacca Morte (allow 1h+ return, to allow for getting lost…). *IGN map 4254 ET*

Equipment: see page 12; no special equipment needed, except warm clothing in cool weather

Transport: 🚗 car to/from the Sentier des Tafoni nature trail: leave the D386 1km north of l'Ospédale, turning left for 'Agnarone, Cartalavonu, Tavogna'. Referring to the 🚗 symbols on the map, fork left (200m), left (400m), and left again (for 'Le Refuge, Cartalavonu'). Park on the right, 500m uphill. For 🚌 information, see page 132 under 'Walk 2'.

Refreshments:
Le Refuge at Cartalavonu (page 31)

Points of interest:
forestry nature trail
tafoni — rocks eroded into whimsical shapes
nearby Barrage de l'Ospédale

One sign points the way to a 'Vue Panoramique' over the gulfs of Valinco and Porto-Vecchio. Another sign indicates a path to Punta di a Vacca Morta (Dead Cow Peak). If the day is fine, and you decide to climb to the summit, allow a good

27

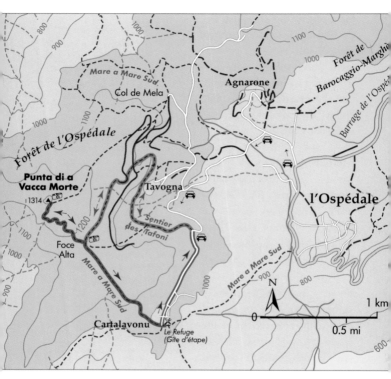

35 minutes to puzzle your way up: there are many paths, and the cairns tend to peter out! (There is another path to the top further down the northbound Mare a Mare — 100m before the Mare a Mare leaves the forestry track for a footpath on the right. This also divides into many cairned paths, but they all lead to

the top.) From the summit, you enjoy a 360° pano-
rama over southern Corsica.

A third sign at the col points to the Mare a
Mare route south via Cartalavonu. This steep,
narrow route, well waymarked with the orange
flashes of the Mare a Mare, runs down through
holm oaks and pines to Cartalavonu … and Le
Refuge, the splendid restaurant described overleaf. Stronger
walkers may like to descend here, have a meal, and then walk
back down the road (1km) to their cars.

Otherwise, from Foce Alta return the same way to the **start
of the nature trail (1h10min)** and drive to Le Refuge.

Barrage de l'Ospédale

Le Refuge

This tucked-away restaurant is a real find! It's a popular *gîte d'étape* for walkers on the Mare a Mare Sud; otherwise it's likely

LE REFUGE
Forêt de l'Ospédale, Cartalavonu
(04 95 70 00 39
closed 6/11-15/3 and Sun in winter, otherwise non-stop service from noon; no credit cards €€

entrées include the delicious *salade refuge* (Corsican charcuterie and sheeps' cheeses, pine nuts and pickles — often called *salade bergère; see page 103), salade de croustillant* (grilled goats' cheese), marinated leeks, terrine of wild boar with onion chutney

traditional main courses feature canneloni with *brocciu* cheese, aubergines stuffed with *brocciu* and basil, veal or wild boar sautéed in a sauce of Corsican wine and tomato, Corsican-style tripe (in a tomato/wine sauce with herbs), pasta with Corsican veal, grilled steaks or pork

sweets like chestnut cake (not wheat-free, alas), *fiadone* (see page 123), nougat glacé with raspberry sauce, crème brulée with a chestnut sauce — and of course a selection of Corsican cheeses

good **wine list** — try the Costa Rossa Figari red

Le Refuge

that only locals and French tourists make their way here (it's mentioned in the Routard and Michelin Guide Verte). The ambiance is very casual and rustic, but the food is brilliant — really high-class cooking of

restaurants

eat

Corsican specialities, all supervised by Marie, who founded the restaurant some 15 years ago.

The dishes are all à la carte. We've shown some offerings from the *winter* menu — the summer list is double this size and also offers a special 'menu' at 45 € per person. While this is quite pricey, it *is* rather special. It is only available by reservation, for a minimum of four people, and is centred around *porcelet* (suckling pig) or *agneau de lait* (baby milk-fed lamb), which is flamed at the table, then removed to the kitchen and carved. The price also includes a sweet or cheese course and a bottle of wine.

Served with the cheese is the very typical Corsican fig chutney — very easy to make at home. Walnuts are a nice touch too.

Corsican fig chutney *(confiture de figues)*

Wash the figs in cold water, drain and dry. Pierce them liberally with a small skewer. Place in a heavy-bottomed casserole and add the sugar, being sure to cover all the fruit.

Split the vanilla pod in two and cut into pieces. Sprinkle over the fruit, then add about two glasses of water. Bring just to the boil, then take off the scum. Cook over a very low heat for about 3 hours, removing the scum from time to time.

Drain the figs and ladle them into sterilised jam jars, pour the syrup on top and let them cool.

<u>Ingredients (for about 4 jars)</u>
1.5 kg green figs
600 g caster sugar
1 vanilla pod

recipes

eat

Wild boar stew with ceps *(civet de sanglier aux cèpes)*

This is not Marie's recipe, but one we've concocted based on her ingredients. Boar is pictured here, but she uses the same sauce for Corsican veal; we like it with venison.

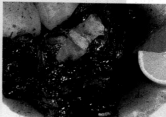

Cut the meat into 2.5 cm cubes. Marinate overnight with the following 8 listed ingredients (from carrot to red wine). The next day, remove the meat from the marinade and set aside. Then strain all the vegetables from the marinade and reserve. In a saucepan, reduce the wine by half, skimming off impurities.

Preheat the oven to 160°C/325°F/gas mark 4. Dry the meat on paper towels, season, and brown all sides in olive oil in a heavy skillet. Transfer to a casserole. Swish the reserved vegetables around in the skillet until they are lightly caramelised, then transfer to the casserole.

Pour in the wine reduction, stock and tomatoes. Stir in the tomato paste. Make sure the meat is covered (add more wine if necessary!). At this stage we tend to add another teaspoon of Corsican herbs. Bring to a simmer, cover, and transfer to the oven.

When meat is almost cooked (2h or so), add the mushrooms and cook for another 20min, then remove from the oven. Strain all the liquid into a saucepan and reduce to the desired volume (generally by at least half). Pour the sauce over the meat and heat the lot gently until warmed through.

Ingredients (for 4 people)
1.2 kg wild boar (or venison or hare)
1 carrot, peeled and diced
1 stalk celery, peeled and diced
1 onion, peeled and diced
5 cloves garlic
6 juniper berries, crushed
2 bay leaves, crushed
1 tsp Corsican herbs
500 ml red wine
500 ml stock
400 g fresh or 100 g dry ceps (porcini mushrooms)
1 tsp tomato purée
75 g tomatoes, peeled and diced
olive oil for browning

The Massif of Bavella, with its towering pink walls and magnificent pine woods, has a magnetic, irresistible beauty. This walk to the edge of the southern massif is shady and undemanding — perfect for a warm day. But it's not lacking in drama — you can either admire the 'shell-hole' from a distance, or climb right up to it!

bavella: trou de la bombe

WALK

3

Start out at the **Auberge du Col de Bavella** (200m east downhill from the parking area at the col). Take the forestry track opposite the *auberge*, marked with the red and white flashes of the **GR20** and signposted 'Paliri'. There is a **fountain** here. From the outset you have a superb view that stretches to the sea, but it's the formidable wall of rocky pink crags bulging out of the landscape and blocking your way that holds your attention. Pines wood the sheer slopes. From here the modest settlement of Bavella is concealed by woods.

Distance: 6km/3.7mi; 2h

Grade: fairly easy, with overall ascents of under 150m/500ft; agility is required on the approach to the Trou de la Bombe. *IGN map 4253 ET*

Equipment: see page 12; walking boots recommended, but not mandatory

Transport: 🚌 or 🚐 (see page 132) to/from the Auberge du Col (200m east of the Col de Bavella)

Refreshments:
Auberge du Col de Bavella (see page 39)

Points of interest:
Aiguilles de Bavella
rock formations, including the Trou de la Bombe

Some 600m/yds from the *auberge,* fork right uphill (**10min**) on a path waymarked with red paint. This rises gently through ferns and pines. Ten minutes uphill you meet a crossing path, where 'Bavella par la Chapelle' is signposted to the right (you will return this way). Turn left here, for '**Compuleddu**' and '**Pianona**'. Two minutes later, at another fork, 'Trou de la Bombe' is signposted down to the left. Although that is our destination, first we'll make a short detour to a pretty viewpoint.

Fork *right uphill* here for '**Pianona**', following orange way-

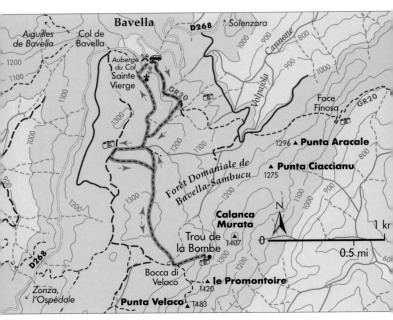

marks. An easy ascent of eight minutes brings you to a crossing track at the top of a rise, at the setting shown overleaf, a **grassy plateau** (**30min**) from where you look out to the spiky Aiguilles (Needles) de Bavella.

Turn left on the track and, three minutes later, fork left on a lesser track (*not* waymarked). This narrows to a path and brings you back to the main 'Trou de la Bombe' path in four minutes: turn right on this wider, crossing path. The gentle undulations of this red-waymarked path bring you to a barrage of signposts

Torou de la Bombe

View towards the cloud-covered Bavella needles from the grassy plateau

at the **Bocca di Velaco** (**55min**). Cairned paths (*not* signposted) lead almost straight ahead from this pleasant clearing up to the jagged heights of Punta Velaco and le Promontoire. But we turn *left* here. After about seven minutes, take a path climbing up to the right (red waymarking on trees). In two minutes you're just below the 'shell-hole' (**Trou de la Bombe**; **1h05min**). Red flashes show the best way to the hole itself, if you're brave.

Back at the Bocca di Velaco, follow 'Bavella par la Chapelle', retracing your outgoing route. Just after crossing a stream, you are back at the sign for the Pianona detour. Go right, then, two minutes later, turn left, now following red and orange flashes to the **Chapelle de la Sainte Vierge** (**1h50min**) and **Bavella** (**2h**).

Auberge du Col de Bavella

If you love mountains inns, then you'll love the Auberge du Col. But *do* work up an appetite before arriving; this *gîte d'étape* caters for walkers, and the portions of traditional, hearty Corsican fare are *huge*. There is a large airy dining room and a lovely terrace, but outside the main season, we prefer the more intimate snug (where they also sell Corsican goodies).

AUBERGE DU COL
200m east of the Col de Bavella
℡ 04 95 72 09 87
www.auberge-bavella.com
closed mid-Nov to mid-Mar, otherwise open daily, all day €–€€
menus at 15 €, 22 €

for **entrées** there are salads, various pâtés, charcuterie of the house, Bavella ham with melon

Corsican specialities: soup with ham bone, omelette with *brocciu*, aubergines or courgettes stuffed with *brocciu*, Corsican-style veal tripe, stew of haricot beans with *panzetta* (see page 130), wild boar stew with polenta, veal sauté with penne, Corsican veal cutlets with honey sauce, roast goat

all kinds of **pastas**

Corsican **cheeses** and sweets like chestnut or pear tart, apple cake

good **wine list**

restaurants

eat

Veal cutlets in honey sauce with mushrooms
(côtelettes de veau corse au miel)

First prepare the sauce: in a saucepan, reduce the stock to half. In another pan, cook the sugar and vinegar until the mixture caramelises. Add the stock, honey, salt and pepper to taste, and cornflour. Bring to a boil, then set aside.

Fry the cutlets in olive oil (or grill if you prefer) and keep warm.

Sauté the mushrooms in butter, then add the honey sauce to the mushrooms and heat through. Pour over the cutlets and sprinkle with parsley.

Veal cutlet in honey sauce at the Auberge de Bavella, where the veal is cooked on a wood fire. Honey is a very popular ingredient on the island, and in all France only Corsican honeys carry an AOC designation. Some Corsican honeys are really strong. Since Corsican veal is more strongly flavoured than pen-reared meat, it might be better, back home, to use this sauce on pork cutlets.

Ingredients (for 4 people)
4 large veal or pork cutlets
2 garlic cloves, crushed
150 g buttom mushrooms
400 ml veal or chicken stock
50 g granulated sugar
50 ml red wine vinegar
2 tbsp chestnut (or strongly-flavoured) honey
1 tsp cornstarch, dissolved in water
fresh parsley
salt and pepper to taste
olive oil and butter for frying

recipes

eat

The *auberge* claims to be the only establishment on the island that makes this pie. We've tried to match the taste; the consistency is like mince pie. In fact we plan to try substituting 100 g mincemeat next time, to make a 'Christmas chestnut tart', flavouring it with brandy or rum instead of vanilla.

Chestnut tart
(tarte aux châtaignes)

We've used gram (chick pea) flour for the base — a crispy pastry that doesn't need pre-baking. Use any base you like.

Mix the sugar with the flour and sift. Bring the flour/sugar and butter or margarine together with cold hands or in a food processor. When it has the consistency of breadcrumbs, mix in the water and lightly knead into a ball. Wrap in cling film and set aside for 30min.

Meanwhile, preheat the oven to 180°C/ 325°F/gas mark 4 and grease a 20 cm/ 8 in circular loose-bottomed tin.

Stir together the chestnuts, sugar, honey and vanilla. Add the eggs and mix well.

Roll out the pastry, line the tin, bottom and sides, and pour in the filling. Bake for about 30-40min, until a toothpick inserted into the centre comes out clean. Sprinkle with powdered sugar to serve. Good warm or cold — with cream or ice cream.

Ingredients
(for 10 servings)

for the base:
100 g gram flour
1 tbsp caster sugar
50 g butter or hard margarine
1-2 tbsp cold water

for the filling:
400 g prepared chestnuts, roughly chopped
3 tbsp caster sugar
2 large eggs, beaten
1 tsp vanilla
3 tbsp chestnut honey

to serve:
icing sugar

This easy out-and-back (or alternative, circular) walk puts you into the holiday mood straight away. It gives you a taste of the beaches to come, and takes you through picturesque countryside. In spring you'll be intoxicated by the sweet-smelling *maquis,* when the hillsides are ablaze with a riot of brightly-coloured flowers.

pointe de la parata

WALK

The walk begins at the **Pointe de la Parata**. This rocky promontory is the site of a 17th-century Genoese tower, built as a defence against the Moors. Beyond the point lie the Iles Sanguinaires, a group of sharp granite islets. If you want a *very* easy walk — just a stroll — walk round the tower, or climb up to it.

For the main walk, take the gravelly path at the left-hand side of the restaurant. Immediately you're swallowed up in *maquis*.* In spring an array of flowers holds your attention all along, and yellow spiny broom lights up the hillsides. You head round into an aquamarine-coloured bay, set at the foot of dark green hills. Vivid carmine *Lampranthus* covers the banks.

Distance: up to 13.5km/8.4mi; 4h45min (the walk can be shortened at any point)

Grade: easy, but some thorny scrub on route. No shade on beaches, can be very hot. Overall ascents/descents of 150m/490ft. IGN map 4153 OT

Equipment: as page 12; light shoes, sun protection, bathing things and plenty of water recommended

Transport: 🚗 or 🚌 (see page 132) to/from the Pointe de la Parata

Refreshments: restaurants at the Pointe de la Parata and along the D111 (see Alternative walk)

Alternative walk: Pointe de la Parata — Capigliolo — D111 (10km/6.2mi; 2h20min; grade as main walk, but with overall ascents and descents of 250m/820ft). Access by bus as above. Follow the main walk to Capigliolo, climb the motorable track up to the D111b, and turn right downhill to the D111 (bus stop and restaurant — see page 46).

Points of interest: seascapes, coastal flora, Genoese tower

*In spring and early summer this path — one of the loveliest stretches on the walk — may be overgrown with head-high lacerating *maquis*. If it looks impassable when you visit, walk or drive 700m back along the D111: 200m before the tennis courts (where you could park) walk uphill to a large rectangular ruin with two doorways and join the walk at the 10min-point.

43

Anse de
Minaccia

Capigliolo

Plage de
St-Antoine

Bocca di
Canareccia

100

200

282
▲
Punta
Alta

D111b

221
▲
Punta
di Frati

100

Sémaphore

Route interdite

D111

Le
Weekend

Pointe de
la Corba

Golfe d' Ajaccio

Tennis courts

N

1 km

Tour de
la Parata

Îles Sanguinaires

0

0.5 mi

Rising to a large rectangular **ruin with two doorways** (an old rifle range; **10min**), you will see your ongoing route ahead: a dirt track following the west coast. Make your way over to it, maybe in the company of the odd car bumping along to one of the flower-filled weekend retreats. After crossing a low crest above the **Pointe de la Corba** (**30min**), you look down into a small rocky cove. The track descends to it, but you bear right, keeping along the wide path. Lizards galore dart across your path, as you brush your way through flowers.

As you cross over a ridge (**1h**), a superb view greets you: two beautiful beaches rest in the now-flat coastline: the first is small and circular, the second large and sweeping. The white sand glares in the sunlight. An open grassy valley, sheltered by high rocky hills, empties out into the bay. The arm of the cape rolls out to the left. Descending, you soon come to a track above the first cove, to find the holiday hamlet of **Capigliolo**. Make your way down to the beach, the **Plage de St-Antoine** (**1h12min**). From here head inland, if you're doing the Alternative walk.

To continue along the coast, squeeze through the rocks at the end of this blinding-white cove, and carry on up the bank. Just beyond the next cove, a clearer path leads you to the **Anse de Minaccia** (**1h25min**) in unspoilt countryside. It's possible to continue along the coast for another hour or more, to take in more inviting, usually-deserted coves. But the main walk ends here: return the same way to the **Pointe de la Parata** (**2h50min**) — or take the inland route via the track from Capigliolo, to emerge near a bus stop and Le Weekend, our recommended restaurant.

Le Weekend

This restaurant is almost opposite the D111b where the Alternative walk emerges — it's just a little to the east, on the sea side of the road. While à la carte dishes (and the wines) are fairly expensive, there is an economical luncheon menu at 20 € for any *two* courses.

So treat yourself: the elegant blue and white dining room, with views to the Iles Sanguinaires and the Pointe de la Parata, is delightful and very relaxing. The décor is unusual, too — with a USA/1920s theme and subdued music to match. Although fish and seafood are the speciality, there are some interesting meat dishes.

LE WEEKEND
at the km 7 marker on the D111
(Route des Iles Sanguinaires)
(04 95 52 01 39
lunch and dinner; closed Tue, Wed
and 1-15 Nov €€-€€€ (but a lunch
menu at 20 €)

entrées feature 8 different cold plates, including oysters and pâté de foie gras; there are two hot entrées — home-made fish soup and *beignets* with a *coulis* of tomatoes (see opposite)

mains include 5-6 kinds of fresh **fish** — grilled or poached: cod, sea bass, daurade, various species of sea bream, rascasse, etc; also **seafood**: lobster, crawfish, crayfish, giant prawns; **meats**: duck with red fruits, lamb shanks with garlic and *pistou*, fillet of beef cooked over a wood fire with foie gras and a sauce of wine and beef marrow

Grilled darne of cod at Le Weekend, served with gooseberries in a white wine sauce

restaurants

eat

Courgette fritters
(beignets de courgettes)

First prepare the batter: in a bowl mix the flour, 1 tbsp of oil, 200 ml warm water, the egg yolk and a pinch of salt. The batter should be elastic but not too runny. Cover and set aside for 2 hours.

Make our quick 'cheat's' sauce: sweat the garlic and shallot in the oil, add the other ingredients and simmer for about 20-30min. It should be very thick and fairly sweet, *not* acidic. Remove the bouquet garni, toss in some more fresh parsley and mint if you like, and set aside to cool. (Some recipes add sliced olives and fresh anchovies.)

Wash and clean the courgettes, but do not peel. Slice them about 7 mm (1/4 in) thick and place in a wide, deep dish. Add 2 tsp of oil, the lemon juice, parsley, mint, salt and pepper. Mix and let marinate for an hour, then remove.

Beat the egg white into stiff peaks and fold into the batter. Heat the oil to 175°C/350°F. Mix the courgettes in the batter and fry until golden and puffed up. Drain on paper towels and serve at once, very hot.

Ingredients (for 4 people)
for the fritters
5 smallish thin-skinned
   courgettes
200 g flour
500 ml sunflower or similar oil
1 egg, separated
juice of 1 lemon
4 sprigs flat parsley, minced
4 fresh mint leaves, minced
salt and ground pepper
for the sauce (coulis)
400 g tinned tomatoes
20 ml olive oil
2 garlic cloves, crushed
1 shallot, minced
2 tsp sugar
1 tsp tomato concentrate
1 bouquet garni

recipes

eat

The cascading Agnone River is the essence of this walk, bounding downstream below Corsica's fifth-highest peak. An apron of pines covers Monte d'Oro's lower slopes, but the valley is home to a splendid beech forest. Of all these beautiful gifts of nature, it's the river you'll remember ... and the dazzling Cascades des Anglais.

cascades des anglais

WALK

The walk begins at la Foce, almost opposite 'A Muntagnera'. Follow the forestry track downhill. Monte d'Oro (2389m/7835ft) soon appears through the beech trees, filling in this picture. Its naked rocky crown rises high above the pine wood patching its inclines. When the track makes a U-bend down to the right, keep straight ahead on a path — to the crystal-clear, bubbly river, with its green and alluring pools. There is a **bridge** here, and a seasonal **kiosk** (**15min**). The GR20 from Vizzavona crosses the bridge here, while the 'Sentier des Cascades' (nature trail) keeps to the north side of the river.

Remaining on the south side of the river, we now follow the GR. There is no single clearly-trodden path, so follow the red and white way-marks carefully. The Agnone bounces down the valley

Distance: 4km/2.5mi; 1h05min

Grade: moderate, but you must be sure-footed; descent/ascent of about 100m/300ft. IGN map 4251 OT

Equipment: see page 12; walking boots recommended — or stout shoes; bathing things in hot weather

Transport: 🚗 or 🚐 (see page 132); park/alight almost opposite 'A Muntagnera' at la Foce, east of the Col de Vizzavona on the N193. Or 🚂 (see page 132 and the Alternative walk below).

Refreshments:
Hotel du Monte d'Oro (see page 56)

Alternative walk: Start the walk from the railway station: turn right uphill on the road, to the signposted 'Sentier des Cascades' (also the 'GR20 Nord') — on the right, just before a chapel. Carefully follow the red and white GR waymarking (and wooden posts with a pine tree motif) to the bridge over the Agnone, cross it, and pick up the main walk at the 15min-point (add 30min to all times).

Optional extension: Old CAF refuge (8.5km/5.3mi; 3h50min in total). See notes on page 52. A wonderful hike for the energetic.

Points of interest:
Agnone river, local history

Cascades des Anglais

alongside you, one falls after another — the **Cascades des Anglais**. At the top of the last cascade, a large **cairn (30min)** on the left alerts you to your route back to la Foce. *(If you first want to press ahead up the valley, see overleaf.)*

Turn left and head back southeast above the GR, contouring through a cairned rock chaos and then beech woods. After 15 minutes, at a Y-fork, turn right, up to the top of the ridge and the ruined fort shown at the right, which you reach in just a couple of minutes. Follow the good path (yellow waymarks) east along the ridge, and be sure to fork right after a few minutes, down to the **N193**. You emerge almost opposite the entrance to the **Hotel Monte d'Oro** — just, we hope, in time

The remains of the old French fort on the ridge above the Col de Vizzavona; its stones were used to rebuild the Chapel of Our Lady of the Snows (see page 55)

for lunch. A Muntagna and the start of the track down to the Cascades is just to the left.

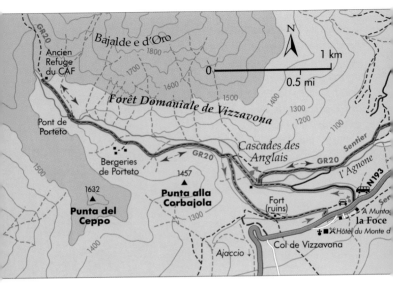

Alternative walk to the old CAF refuge: Continue ahead at the 30min-point, still on the GR20. The route is very steep at times; sometimes you'll be using all fours. Green lichen illuminates the surrounding rock; under direct sunlight it glows with the fluorescence of a highlighter pen. Ignore a turn-off to the left at the **Bergeries de Porteto**, then cross the river on a **footbridge** (**1h40min**), above a small but thundering waterfall.

Continue as far as you like — perhaps to the scant remains of the old French Alpine Club (CAF) **refuge** (**2h**), where the spring snow-line is not far out of reach. Just below this small crumbled rock shelter is the largest waterfall in the valley.

Vizzavona railway station

You're completely encircled by mountains. In the hills behind la Foce, the Monte Renoso chain may still be wearing a mantle of snow.

Heading back, don't miss the beryl-green pools that lie concealed in the valley floor; some are magnificent. But if you decide to swim, make sure they're safe; the current can be very strong. Return to the kiosk at the **bridge** in 1h30min (**3h30min**), then retrace your steps to **la Foce** (**3h50min**). Or cross the bridge and follow the GR/nature trail to **Vizzavona** (**4h15min**), where the railway station and a couple of hotels are just downhill to the left or you can catch a bus 10 minutes uphill to the right.

Hôtel du Monte d'Oro

This hotel, run by the same family for just over 100 years, was originally built to house engineers piercing the 4km-long tunnel for the railway (see page 125). It became a hotel in 1880 and was bought by the present owners in 1904 (the *refuge* on the main road also belongs to them).

The first visitors were wealthy people

The dining room at the Hôtel du Monte d'Oro — unchanged since the 1880s

HÔTEL DU MONTE D'ORO
Col de Vizzavona
(04 95 47 21 06
www.monte-oro.com
'officially' open from 1 May to 30 Sep, but usually open from Easter until at least mid-Oct -€€

trout (locally caught) is a speciality — bleu, meunière, with pine nuts (see page 57)

Corsican **soup**, **omelettes**, **salads**, **charcuterie** for a lighter meal

meats include steaks, pork, veal, duck in honey sauce (see page 56)

good selection of **sweets** and **wines** (especially from around Ajaccio)

restaurants

eat

from Bastia, Ajaccio, Paris … and England — who saw it as a low-key hill station from where they could enjoy pleasant shaded walks — hence the name 'Waterfalls of the English'.

Our Lady of the Snows

The place is wonderful — a step back in time to a more leisurely era. The (non-smoking) dining room — like a garden, full of plants — is still as it was at end of 19th century, with turned wood chairs, thick white napkins and silver cutlery. You will enjoy fine, traditional Corsican cooking. If you're enjoying a coffee in the lounge afterwards, ask to see the book of the hotel's history; the notes are in English and French and make interesting reading.

One of the stories concerns the chapel of Our Lady of the Snows in the hotel grounds (where Sunday services are still held). During World War Two the original, wooden chapel was used by occupying Italian troops to house their mules. When the chaplain of the Italian Army came to the hotel, Mme Plaisant showed him how it had been desecrated. He evicted the animals, burned the chapel down (to purify it), and had the Army rebuild it in stone. The stone came from the 17th-century French fort in the photograph on page 53, which we pass near the end of the walk. In fact there was a 16th-century pilgrimage chapel up by the fort, dedicated to St Peter. So, as the history poignantly says, 'the stones returned to their original religious significance'.

In 1940 Ajaccio's military hospital was moved to the hotel. Due to Corsica's resistance, it was the first French territory to be liberated. After the war, German prisoners helped to rebuild the hotel and after the war came back to visit the owners and introduce their families.

The hotel uses its own citrus- and *maquis*-flavoured honey for this dish; 'Monsieur' has been passionate about bee-keeping since reading Maetterlink's *The Life of Bees* many years ago. Unfortunately, they only produce enough for their own needs.

Duck breast with honey sauce (magret de canard au miel)

Fry the mushrooms gently in butter for 15min, turning once or twice. Set aside and keep warm. Cook the duck in a separate, heavy skillet,

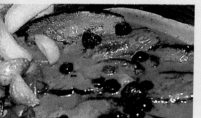

having first pricked the skin to avoid bursting: fry skin side down at a very high heat for 6min, then turn and fry more gently for another 4min with the crushed garlic cloves. Season, remove from pan and keep warm. (After 10min, slice quite thinly and pour the juices back into the skillet.)

Ingredients (for 4 people)

4 duck breasts, preferably French
4 tbsp clear aromatic honey
150 ml duck or chicken stock
2 tbsp raspberry vinegar
1 box 'fruits of the forest'
400 g fresh ceps (porcini mushrooms), or 100 g dry
2 cloves garlic, crushed
1 tsp tomato paste
75 g tomatoes, peeled and diced
salt, freshly-ground pepper
2 tbsp butter, in small pieces

Put half the fruits, the tomatoes, tomato paste and garlic in a saucepan with the stock and boil rapidly to reduce to half. Put this reduction into the skillet and bring to a simmer. Add the honey and let it caramelise slightly. Then stir in the vinegar, strain and re-season. Add the rest of the fruit and heat through. Add the butter bit by bit, whisking to a fairly thick, glossy sauce. Stir in the mushrooms just before serving.

recipes

eat

Trout with pine nuts *(truites aux pignons)*

Preheat the oven to 190°C/375°F/gas mark 5. Season the trout and place, whole, in an ovenproof dish with the onion, herbs, lemon slice and wine. Cover with foil and bake for about 20min, until tender.

Remove the trout from the baking dish; set aside and keep warm. (You may prefer at this stage to fillet the fish; at the Hôtel Monte d'Oro it is served whole.) Strain the cooking liquid; you should be left with 150 ml — add some water or fish stock if short.

Melt the butter in a saucepan over a low heat, sprinkle in the flour bit by bit and, stirring vigorously, cook to a paste. Slowly add the cooking liquid, stirring constantly to avoid lumps, and bring to the boil. Add the cream (still stirring), and bring to the boil again. Reduce the heat, stir in the pine nuts and warm through. Season.

Pour the sauce over the fish and sprinkle with parsley. Best served with *fluffy* rice, as here at the Hôtel Monte d'Oro! At the moment it is fashionable on Corsica to serve a rice 'timbale' (moulded, as in the photograph on page 25), which usually leaves it as appealing as set concrete...

Ingredients (for 4 people)

4 trout, about 200 g each
200 m dry white wine
1 small onion, minced
1 bay leaf, some fresh thyme, parsley and a slice of lemon
25 g butter
1 tbsp flour
150 ml single cream
150 g pine nuts
salt and freshly-ground black pepper
chopped parsley to garnish

This tour of the three Venacos is a lovely complement to a journey on the little train. For the energetic, the whole 'Venachese' area, at the heart of the Parc Natural Régional, is a walking centre *par excellence,* a crossroads of the long-distance Mare a Mare Nord and many shorter, locally-marked routes (Sentiers du Pays).

the venacos

WALK

Start out at **Poggio-Riventosa station**: rather than following the road uphill into Poggio, take the path uphill through the woods , cutting a big loop off the road. When you come back onto the D140, follow it 400m to the right, into **Poggio-di-Venaco (20min)**.

With your back to the **war memorial**, walk down the narrow road ahead, at the right of an electricity transformer (signposted 'Casanova, Corte'). There is an orange flash of the Mare a Mare Nord on an electricity pole at the right. You pass below a **cemetery** on the left. When the road makes a U-turn to the right two minutes later, go left downhill on path (orange flash). Cross a burbling stream on a **footbridge** and rise up through a ferny dell. Approaching Casanova, veer right on a cart track and pass to the left of a stone hut.

Distance: 8km/5mi; 2h50min

Grade: moderate, with ascents/descents of about 400m/1300ft overall. *IGN map 4251 OT*

Equipment: as page 12; stout shoes recommended

Transport: 🚌 to Poggio-Riventosa *(request stop!)*; return from Venaco (see page 133). Or 🚗 to one of the stations and take the train to start the walk or to get back to your car.

Shorter circuit: quite easy; 6km/3.7mi; 2h; 🚗 or 🚌. Follow the main walk (omitting the detour into Riventosa) to Santo-Pietro. Have lunch, then return to Riventosa. Walk up past the church and the fine view towards Corte, then curl down to the D40. Turn left and, after 30m/yds, fork right on a footpath. This soon meets the road and your short-cut path back to the railway station.

Refreshments en route:
Gîte d'étape in Poggio-di-Venaco
Gîte d'étape and hotel in Casanova
Le Torrent (see page 64) and Le Petit Bosquet in Santo Pietro
Bar/Restaurant de la Place (see page 65) and a couple of bar/cafés and shops in Venaco

Points of interest:
high-mountain surroundings at the centre of the Regional Natural Park

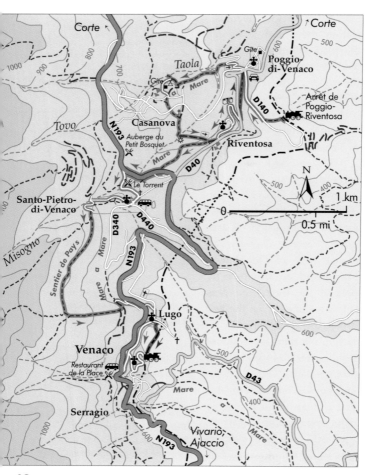

You come to the end of a road, which you will follow to the left uphill. But first walk down to the pretty **Ruisseau de Taola** (**40min**): either go straight along the cart track to a dam, or take a path half-right, just where the road begins.

The road passes a camp site on the left and a **fountain** on the right, as you skirt **Casanova**, with its traditional slate-roofed buildings. Go straight over a crossroads, onto a cobbled path and, almost at once, turn left on a crossing path. Rise up to a road and cross it (**45min**). Ignore a track to the left (by a **tomb** with cypresses) and keep ahead towards Riventosa, which rises above to left, spread out along a ridge. Contour through tall grass, then cross another tinkling stream on a **footbridge** (**50min**) and pass the **Moulin de Riventosa** on the right.

A shady track takes you up to **Riventosa**. Walk to the right of the **cemetery**, then continue to the right uphill on a concrete road. After 20-

Top: detail on a tomb in Poggio-di-Venaco; below: the Ruisseau de Taola

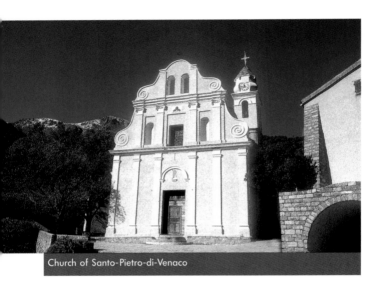

Church of Santo-Pietro-di-Venaco

30m the Mare a Mare turns sharp right to Santo-Pietro (your ongoing route). But first, to see pretty Riventosa and enjoy a fine view, continue on to the main D40 (**1h**; **tap**, **war memorial**), then walk up the cobbled road, at the right of the **church**. At a Y-fork, go right on a narrow road, until you have a tremendous view towards Corte.

From here turn back to the orange waymarks of the Mare a Mare and follow it to the **N193** (**1h15min**). Turn right, then *ignore* the Mare a Mare waymarks leading directly to the church in Santo-Pietro: keep along the N193 for a short distance, and you will come to the entrance drive to the hotel Le Torrent on the left. This is our recommended restaurant, housed in the old Chateau Pozzo di Borgo. (A little further along the N193, on the right, is the Auberge du Petit Bosquet.)

From Le Torrent continue on the narrow D340 behind the hotel (orange waymarks), crossing a stream and passing a **war memorial** on the left. You come to the lovely church at Santo-Pietro. From here the easiest option is just to follow the Mare a Mare to Venaco, but it is mostly along the same narrow road. Our suggested way on to Venaco takes a somewhat higher route: walk up the narrow lane at the right of the church, by the **fountain** and **walkers' signboard**. When you come to a fork, where a right turn leads to 'Coto Pratu' (a lovely high-level walk described in *Landscapes of Corsica*), go left for '**Venaco**' (**1h40min**). The route (orange waymarked 'Sentier de Pays' rises 100m and contours at about 900m, to a crossroads of paths. Go left here, down to the **N193** (**2h20min**), where you pick up the Mare a Mare once more.

Follow the orange waymarks down into **Lugo**. If you don't want to visit Venaco, you can take a short-cut to the railway station: fork right on a stone-laid path behind the **church**, down to the railway *line*. Walk along the track to the right for 150m, to **Venaco station** (**2h35min**). If you *do* want to visit Venaco, from Lugo's church follow the D340 south to a Y-fork (just before the **church**). Go right, uphill, here (the road to the left leads down to the station). The Restaurant de la Place is on the far side of the N193 in the centre of **Venaco**, just to the left. From there descend the same way, to walk back to the **railway station** (**2h50min**).

Le Torrent

The IGN map shows a château at Poggio, locating it due east of the church. Expecting to see a tower or at least a turret or two, we just assumed it was in ruins when it never materialised over the years. But lunching at Le Torrent, we realised we had found it! The building dates from the late 19th century; its interesting history is on the web site (in French).

Le Torrent, once the château of the Pozzo di Borgo family

LE TORRENT
D340, Santo-Pietro-di-Venaco (also an entrance drive off the N193)
(**04 95 47 00 18**
www.letorrent.com
daily except Sun dinner, all year €€-€€€

8 **entrées**, including tart with Corsican herbs, *escargots*, *moules*, local pâté, head-cheese with a nut or raspberry vinegar

5 different fresh **pastas**, including sauces with giant prawns or *brocciu*

brocciu **omelette**

fish: sea bass grilled with fennel or ginger, daurade in white wine or ginger and curry sauce, giant prawns cooked three different ways, trout — grilled or baked and stuffed with *brocciu*

meats: entrecôte, veal chop with sage and lemon, roast milk-fed lamb with Corsican herbs, slivers of chicken — either with ginger and honey, curry and coconut milk, mustard sauce, or lemon and vanilla

small **wine list**

restaurants

eat

An enthusiastic small new management team had just taken over when we visited, and while we dined off Limoges porcelain (!), they fretted over the décor … and the huge pit near the front terrace where they were already stoking the fires for an evening barbecue.

The dining room is non-smoking. At the time of our visit there was no daily 'menu', so our à la carte meal was fairly pricey, but no doubt a reasonably priced menu is now on offer.

Bar/Restaurant de la Place

Totally different from the elegant Torrent, this is a relaxed, inexpensive meeting place on the main square in Venaco, where you can join the locals on the front terrace and watch lorries laden with huge

BAR/RESTAURANT DE LA PLACE
N193, Venaco centre (04 95 47 01 30
closed either Mon or Wed from Nov to April €-€€

'menu corse' at 13 €: three courses with a choice of Corsican charcuterie, Corsican salad or quiche Venaco-style (Venaco is well known for its ewes' milk cheese), followed by cannelloni with *brocciu*, veal stew with olives, or pork cutlets with ceps; Corsican cheeses or dessert of the day

the à la carte menu lists various **entrées**: 6 salads, 10 pizzas, omelettes; **main courses** include entrecôte, lamb chops, slivers (*aiguilettes*) of chicken, or chicken with curry; there are also **pastas**: tagliatelli carbonara or fricassee of tagliatelli with mushrooms

laricio pines trying to negotiate the U-bend.

Very friendly atmosphere; run by a husband and wife team, Michel and Marie Catherine.

Chicken in curry and coconut milk
(poulet au curry et au lait de coco)

First make the curry: heat the coriander and cumin seeds and the cardamom pods to dry them (either under a hot grill, or in a dry skillet, turning constantly for 1min), then mix with the ginger, fresh coriander and garlic. Crush all together until you have a paste, then add the fish sauce. Stir; set aside.

Heat the oil in a wok or large frying pan. Fry the chicken just to seal, then put in the onions and fry for another 2-3min. Add the curry paste and stock; mix well and simmer, covered, for 20min.

Pour in the coconut milk; add a few drops of lemon juice. Stir, then bring to the boil for a few minutes. Turn down the heat and simmer for another 10min, uncovered, to reduce.

Meanwhile, gently fry the spinach in oil for a few minutes. Serve the curry on a bed of basmati rice, decorated with the spinach leaves.

<u>Ingredients (for 4 people):</u>
4 chicken breast fillets, cut into thin strips
2 medium onions, minced
small bag of spinach
500 ml chicken stock
200 ml coconut milk
few drops lemon juice
sesame or peanut oil for frying
salt and pepper

for the curry paste:
1 tsp coriander seeds
2 cardamom pods, crushed
1 tsp ground ginger
2 tbsp fresh chopped coriander
1/2 tsp cumin seeds
2 garlic cloves, minced
2 tbsp Thai fish sauce

recipes

eat

We didn't have the chicken in curry at Le Torrent, but concocted a similar dish later at home which was quite easy to prepare (see opposite).

What we *did* have was leg of lamb in a lovely sauce. To prepare this lamb, stud it with garlic slivers as you would normally, but instead of adding rosemary, first lightly coat the lamb with oil, then roll it in Corsican herbs *(aromates du maquis)*. The lamb should be *completely* covered in the herbs. Roast as normal, then, when it is resting, scrape off some of the roasted herbs, ease out the garlic, and add to the pan juices with some white wine. After slicing the meat, add those juices as well and boil rapidly for a few minutes to reduce a bit.

Along with the lamb they served a *cake:* we didn't know what to expect, but this turned out to be a delicious vegetable 'custard' flavoured with cumin. We've tried to duplicate it below.

Vegetable 'cake' *(cake aux legumes)*, not illustrated

Preheat the oven to 180°C/350°F/gas mark 4. Grease 4 200 ml custard cups. Steam the leek, carrots and onion until tender (about 10min).

Beat the eggs and whisk in the cream and butter until smooth. Stir in the cumin and the cooked vegetables. Season.

Divide into the custard cups and bake in a bain-marie in the lower part of the oven for 40min, or until a knife inserted into the centre comes out clean. Run the knife round the edge of the cups to remove — *carefully!*

Ingredients (for 4 people):
1 leek, sliced
2 carrots, finely sliced
1 medium onion, diced
2 large eggs
2 tbsp heavy cream
2 tbsp unsalted butter, in
    small pieces
1 tsp cumin seeds
salt and pepper

If you've ever driven up the Restonica road with your heart set on walking to the Melo and Capitello lakes, then your heart will probably sink as you near the Pont de Grotelle! 'Flocks' of walkers — like so many sheep — clog the road, all intent on doing the island's best-known hike.

la restonica

WALK

Admittedly, the 'lakes' walk is a *must*. But for those of you who don't like crowds, or who want an easier option, this walk in a grandiose setting is a fine alternative, with many places to relax by the river or throw yourself into one of its emerald-green pools. And our recommended restaurant is just as brilliant as the hike!

Logistics are a problem. The ideal way to do the walk, *easily*, is to just descend from the Pont de Grotelle to the Pont de Frasseta, then continue 8km down the beautiful riverside *road* to the Auberge de la Restonica. Unless you're with friends, you will need a taxi from Corte. (Note that there is also an hotel at the *auberge*.) Otherwise, take a car and do the walk out-and-back the same way.

Distance: 11km/6.8mi; 4h *return*. If you are travelling with friends or a taxi, you can make this a one-way walk either down from the Pont de Grotelle (1h45min) or up from the Pont de Frasseta (2h15min).

Grade: moderate; descent/reascent of 300m/1000ft. You must be sure-footed (a few rock-falls to cross). Can be very cold; don't attempt in unpredictable weather. IGN map 4251 OT

Equipment: as page 12; walking boots, warm clothing, bathing things recommended

Transport: 🚌 to/from the Pont de Grotelle on the Restonica road (D623, 15km from Corte). Or, if you prefer to walk *uphill* first, park at the Pont de Frasseta (just by the rock pinnacle shown opposite; see map).

Refreshments:
Auberge de la Restonica (see page 73), 2km up from Corte, 8km below the Pont de Frasseta; none en route

Points of interest:
Restonica River and surroundings university town of Corte

We **start out** at the **Pont de Grotelle**, in the magical alpine setting shown on page 71. Cross the bridge, then turn right on a path (signpost: '**Pont de Frasseta 1h50min**'). Ample orange flashes, and some cairns, mark the route all the way to your destination — another bridge a little over 5km downstream. Majestic old pines shade the way and frame your photographs up to the peaks and down to the rushing **Restonica River**. The path undulates for most of the way, sometimes crossing fairly steep rock-falls (where cairns indicate the route if the orange-painted rocks have slipped away). After bumbling over a side-stream on 'stepping-stone' *boulders*, with a **waterfall** up to left (**35min**), cross straight over a track. Soon the path is just beside the **river** (**50min**) — a fine place to swim, if you have time.

When you come to a wide **crossing path** (**1h**), follow it to the left, eventually rising to a tiny grassy **plateau** (**1h10min**). From here the path zigzags steeply downhill, crosses two adjacent streams, and then runs through ferns bright with foxgloves in spring. On the final short ascent,

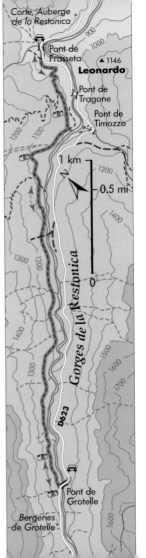

Corte, Auberge de la Restonica

Pont de Frasseta

▲ 1146 **Leonardo**

Pont de Tragone

Pont de Timozzo

1 km

0.5 mi

Gorges de la Restonica

D623

Pont de Grotelle

Bergeries de Grotelle

Pont de Grotelle, at the start of the walk

The bounding Restonica River

you look straight out at **Monte Leonardo**, the rocky pinnacle shown on page 68. At the top of the climb (**1h30min**), just opposite this monolith, you come to a sign: 'Pont de Grotelle 2h', pointing back the way you've come. Turn right at this path junction. Follow the gentle zigzags of the path down to the **Pont de Frasseta** (**1h45min**). From here it's a two hour stroll down the road to the Auberge de la Restonica, but *mind any traffic!* From the *auberge* it's a short 2km hop to Corte, for the train.

Or first return the same way to the **Ponte de Grotelle**, if you left your car there (allow 2h15min, or **4h** in all).

Auberge de la Restonica

Don't miss this restaurant! We took the picture at about 12.30; half an hour later the place was full — not with tourist groups, but just couples or business

people from Corte. The food was fabulous, one of the best meals we've had on the island. We couldn't manage the chestnut parfait, but sampled the chestnut brandy, both sweet *(doux)* and dry *(sec)*; both should be served cold. And the glorious setting, beside the river, is enchanting. *Next time,* we'll spend a night or two at the hotel!

AUBERGE DE LA RESTONICA
Restonica road, 2km up from Corte
℡ 04 95 46 09 58; hotel ℡ 04 95 45 25 25
closed 1 Nov-15 Mar, also Mon outside high season €€

traditional food, wood fire cooked, or snacks by the pool

menu terroir 20 €

entrées: foie gras with myrtle, myrtle aspic and chutney — or pan fried with myrtle wine, Corsican fish soup, duck breast with Corsican honey, roast pigeon with tagliatelli and girolles; regional charcuterie (photo page 8), 'the four seasons' — a mixture of tuna mousse, *tapenade*, tomatoes, and marinated sweet peppers, Corsican soup (see page 102), *brocciu* omelette

fish: small trout — plain, with Corsican herbs, or with garlic, red mullet fillets with scallops, accompanied by blinis of 100% chestnut flour, sea bass grilled with fennel, varied fish *en brochette* with a leek and cream sauce

meat: milk-fed lamb, fillets and faux-fillets, wild boar stew, veal with olives

sweets: hot apple pie, *fiadone* (see page 123), ice cream parfait with chestnuts and chestnut *eau de vie*

the excellent **wine** list offers choices of all Corsican wines listed by region

restaurants

eat

If you don't like garlic, give this dish a miss. But remember that roasted garlic has a mild, almost sweet taste.

Roast leg of lamb with garlic *(gigot d'agneau roti)*

Preheat the oven to 190°C/375°F/gas mark 5. Blanche the garlic and onion for a minute in boiling water (and parboil any another other vegetables you may like to *roast* with the meat), then pan dry and brush lightly with olive oil. Rub the lamb all over with olive oil (again, use a light touch!). Make small incisions in the meat and insert a few slivers of garlic, distributing them evenly.

Place the onion and garlic in the bottom of a roasting pan, then put in a rack and place the meat on top. Roast for 20-25min, or until the meat starts to brown. Now pour over the wine, and continue roasting, basting once or twice, until the meat thermometer registers 140° for medium-rare. Total cooking time should be 2-1/2h but, if you prefer your lamb pink, it should be done in 2h.

Ingredients (for 4 people)

1.5 kg leg of lamb
40 (yes 40!) whole garlic cloves (about 8 full heads)
2 red onions, quartered
1 tsp Corsican herbs
150 ml red wine
salt, freshly ground black pepper
2 tbsp olive oil

Let the meat sit for 10min before carving and add the meat juices to the pan — you may want to boil them up for a few minutes to scrape up all the crunchy bits and reduce. Add more wine if you don't have enough liquid, and reduce again.

recipes

eat

Grilled sea bass with fennel (*loup de mer grillé au fenouil*)

The *auberge* serves their grilled bass covered with poached fennel, but with a sort of hot vegetable 'relish' on the side (see photograph). To make life easier, we've incorporated all the fennel into the relish; serve it atop or beside the fish.

Wash the vegetables. Cut the fennel, leeks and onions into disks 1 cm thick. Pop the leeks, onions, tomatoes and peppers into boiling salted water for a minute or two, then drain and dry.

Quickly fry all the vegetables in a little oil until they just begin to colour. Add the fennel seeds and the chopped herbs and seasoning. Mix well and let this simmer for about 10min. If it begins to dry out, add a little white wine.

While the vegetables are simmering, grill the fish, whole, for about 5min on each side. Carefully transfer the fish to warm plates and serve with the vegetable relish and rice.

Ingredients (for 4 people)

4 small sea bass (about 300 g each) — either packaged or gutted by your fishmonger
4 fennel bulbs
1 leek
12 cherry tomatoes, whole
1/4 each yellow, red and green peppers, finely diced
12 spring onions
8 cloves of garlic
40 ml olive oil
30 ml or so of white wine
1 tsp fennel seeds
2 tbsp each chopped chervil, dill, flat parsley
salt, freshly-ground black pepper

Long a favourite spot for trout fishermen and swimmers, up until 1905 the Cascades d'Aitone also powered three mills for grinding chestnut flour — once a staple of the local diet, and still used today in the better restaurants. This short walk is a delight of waterfalls glistening through a mixed wood of pine, fir, yew and beech.

cascades d'aitone
WALK

The walk from Evisa descends into the Spelunca Gorge from the southern edge of the village, then climbs to Ota, but transport is a major problem. Instead we have chosen this easy route, readily accessible by car. If you're full of energy, there are *two* walks to tackle, in close proximity, before you make your way to Evisa for a meal.

Start out by taking the forestry track at the **signpost** and fork sharp left downhill after about 150m/yds (a right goes to the forestry house). Descend gently to a picnic area with tables, where the Mare a Mare Nord comes in from a track on the left. Steps take you down to the **Piscine d'Aitone (20min)**, a brilliant swimming spot.

Keeping to the left (south) side of the **Ruisseau d'Aitone**, now follow the rough path (agility required) beside the

Distance: 3.2km/2mi; 1h10min

Grade: easy, but you must be agile. Descent/ascent of 70m/230ft. *IGN map 4150 OT*

Equipment: as page 12; strong shoes and bathing things recommended

Transport: 🚗 to/from a parking area *immediately below the track to the Aitone forestry house*, on the north side of the D84 between Evisa and the Col de Vergio. (There are two parking areas for the cascades: park at the higher one, *not* by the fire-point sign 'EVI05'.)

Alternative walk: Sentier de la Sittelle (3.2km/2mi; 1h; easy, very little ascent). This Forestry Department nature trail lies about 2.5km north of the Cascades trail, just north of two 'Paisolu d'Aitone' signs (large parking area). It is waymarked with wooden posts bearing a bird motif (the *sittelle: Sitta Whiteheadi*, the Corsican nuthatch). Beautiful walk through Corsican pines and fir trees. See map.

Refreshments:
hotel-restaurants in Evisa (see recommendation on page 80; *none en route*

Points of interest:
waterfalls, rock pools, Aitone River old mills

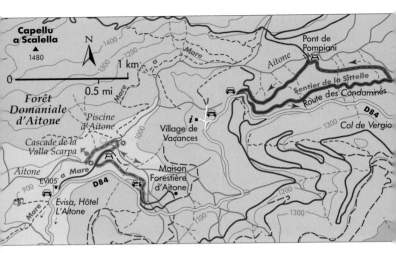

cascading river as far as the signpost '**fin de sentier balisée**'. From here you have a fine view of the largest waterfall, the **Cascade de la Valla Scarpa** (**35min**). One of the mills stood here; now there are only some walls and two millstones.

Return the same way, passing two more ruined mills, to the **parking area** on the D84 (**1h10min**), then drive south to the hotel-restaurant L'Aitone.

L'Aitone

Even on a rainy October day, this friendly restaurant was very warm and welcoming, brightened by rose-coloured place mats and 'Provençal'-style tablecloths. Had the weather been better, we could have enjoyed the fantastic views on offer — from the dining room or the terrace. There is also a pleasant bar area and lounge.

On our previous visit to L'Aitone, we spent a few nights — in mid-November! Dinner was served in the smaller 'snug' with the fireplace — so cosy! It was our first experience of wild boar stew, and it has never tasted better!

Menus vary with the season; we were lucky, as we fancied rabbit, and it's not on the summer menu. They had beautiful roast potatoes, but we choose the polenta, which was served in the same wine sauce as the rabbit.

L'AITONE
D 84, Evisa (04 95 26 20 04
www.hotel-aitone.com
closed Dec, Jan and Mon lunch €–€€

the **à la carte menu** is fairly varied, with 12 entrées; locally-caught trout prepared three ways, sea bass, giant prawns and scallops, beef, veal and 'meat of the day'; Corsican cheeses and a choice of 4 sweets

the **menu** at 16 € (lunch) or 18 € (dinner) is limited: a vegetable entrée, Aitone trout or Corsican omelette (with *brocciu*), vegetables, dessert

the **menu** at 20 € (lunch) or 23 € (dinner) offers a choice of three entrées, three main courses, a cheese course *and* a sweet.

Fried maize polenta at L'Aitone. Chestnut polenta is also popular on the island, but not usually fried.

restaurants

eat

Rabbit sautéed with ceps
(lapin sauté aux cèpes)

Preheat the oven to 190°C/ 375°F/gas mark 5. If you are using dried mushrooms, soak them in warm water for about 30min.

Brown the rabbit pieces in the oil in a heavy casserole, then set aside. Reduce the heat and gently fry the bacon bits, onions and mushrooms until golden. Set aside.

Deglaze the casserole with the wine and stir in the tomato concentrate. Put the meat and mushroom mixture back in, add the thyme, bay, garlic cloves, salt and pepper. Stir to mix. The liquid should just cover the meat (if it does not, add more wine!).

Cover the casserole and cook for 50min-1h, by which time the meat should be falling off the bone. If the sauce is too thin for your taste, strain it into a saucepan and boil rapidly to reduce. Pour over the meat and sprinkle with parsley. Serve with fried polenta (as shown opposite).

Ingredients (for 4 people)

1.5 kg rabbit, jointed
500 g fresh ceps (porcini mushrooms), or 150 g dry, roughly sliced
2 onions, diced
100 g diced streaky bacon, unsmoked
1 bay leaf
2 springs fresh thyme
4 garlic cloves, unpeeled
1 tbsp tomato concentrate
300 ml red wine (or use half chicken stock)
2-3 tbsp olive oil
2 tbsp chopped flat parsley
salt and pepper

recipes
eat

The 'Sentier du Littoral des Agriates' is a 40km-long coastal path stretching from St-Florent to Ostriconi Beach. The land was bought in the 1990s — after fierce opposition and many judicial reviews — by the Conservatoire du Littoral and has been developed and managed for the enjoyment of walkers and others.

sentier du littoral

WALK

9

Whether you follow the whole route suggested here, or only stroll for an hour or so, then stop and swim, this is a lovely walk. Consider driving to the Anse de Fornali to begin: despite all the negotiations and judicial reviews, the wealthy landowners between St-Florent and this cove have managed to bar walkers from their properties which stretch right down to the shore — with jetties, boathouses, and the like. So for the first hour or so, we have to follow a dusty track *behind* their land. (If you read French, just do a web search on 'Sentier du Littoral' to see what was involved!)

Distance: up to 19.5km/12mi; 6h20min *from St-Florent*; 13km/8mi; 4h20min *from the Anse de Fornali*

Grade: easy ups and downs on a good coastal path, but virtually *no shade; adequate sun protection is essential.* IGN map 4348 OT

Equipment: as page 12; stout shoes, ample sun protection, bathing things and *plenty of water* recommended

Transport: 🚌 to/from St-Florent or the Anse de Fornali (saves 2h). By car you can drive along the walking route as far as the 1h-point. The tracks are fairly bumpy, so check your insurance for tyre damage liability, unless you're in a 4WD vehicle.

Refreshments:
bars, cafés, restaurants at St-Florent (see page 87); *none en route*

Points of interest:
coastal flora and fauna
creeks and sandy beaches

Our walk starts in the centre of **St-Florent:** follow the main **D81 towards l'Ile-Rousse.** At the port, take the **footbridge** to the far side of the **Aliso River** and walk across the sandy **Plage de la Roya** to the end. From the end of the beach head inland; then, almost immediately, turn right up a narrow lane, onto a dirt road. Here you'll find a signpost for the **Sentier du Littoral (25min).** When you're above the **Anse de Fornali**

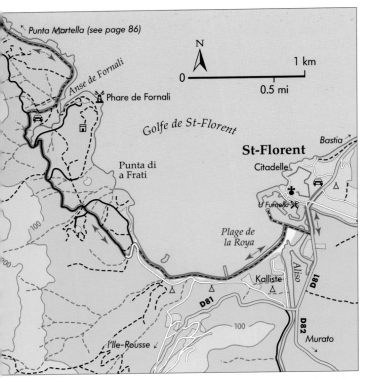

(**1h**), you'll no doubt spot some cars parked over to the right. Take any path from the parking area down to the coastal path proper.

Heading west, you pass below some exquisite properties (some of Europe's wealthiest families have properties here). But

The port at St-Florent

your attention will be no doubt be drawn to the wild flowers, the cloud patterns over Cap Corse, and the endless expanse of crystal-clear aquamarine sea. Just walk as far as you like, stopping to botanise or swim — preferably in a little inlet all your own.

Landmarks are the sandy beach at the mouth of the **Fiume Bughiu (2h)** and the fjord-like inlet at the **Fiume Santu (2h20min)**. From here it's another 50 minutes to the **Punta Mortella (3h10min)**, with its old **Genoese watchtower**. (Nelson was so impressed when his fleet attacked this very tower in 1794 that the so-called Martello towers in Kent and Sussex were

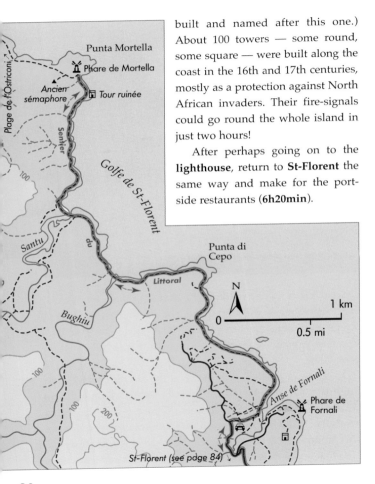

built and named after this one.) About 100 towers — some round, some square — were built along the coast in the 16th and 17th centuries, mostly as a protection against North African invaders. Their fire-signals could go round the whole island in just two hours!

After perhaps going on to the **lighthouse**, return to **St-Florent** the same way and make for the port-side restaurants (**6h20min**).

Punta Mortella
Phare de Mortella
Ancien sémaphore
Tour ruinée
Plage de l'Ostriconi
Sentier
Golfe de St-Florent
Santu
du
Bughiu
Littoral
Punta di Cepo
N
0   0.5 mi   1 km
Anse de Fornali
Phare de Fornali
St-Florent (see page 84)

U Furnellu

Chosen just by chance, this restaurant was fabulous. We could have eaten *everything* on the huge menu — *twice over!* Just showing their specialities takes two columns. Super atmosphere, right at the heart of the port; tables inside or out.

U FURNELLU
Port de Plaisance, Saint-Florent
(**04 95 37 08 46**
closed 1 Nov to 1 Mar, otherwise daily from 11.30 to 23.00 €€

huge menu, which appeals to grown-ups and children alike; **menu corse** at 15 € (children 8 €)

20 different **entrées**: specialities include *brocciu* fritters *(beignets)*, *salade maison* (salad, rice, octopus, giant prawns, *moules*, scallops, lobster), *aubergines à la parmesan*; *croustade de la mer* (scallops, prawns, mussels, fresh mushrooms, sauce), friend fillets of *rouget* on a bed of tomatoes with olive oil

15 **pastas**

dozens of **fish**, with specialities being stuffed squids *(encornets)* in white wine, cognac, tomatoes and butter *(sauce amoricaine)*; fried scallops with a cream of mussels in saffron sauce, sprinkled with parsley; swordfish

20 **pizzas**

8 kinds of **mussels**, including *moules* in Pietra chestnut beer or with *brocciu*, breadcrumbs, garlic and basil

over 20 **Corsican specialites**, including *cassoulet corse* (haricot beans, lamb shanks, *figatellu*, sausage, bacon)

meats 12 different kinds of veal, 12 beef dishes …

sweets and ice creams galore; a speciality is 'Le Petit Napoléon' (see page 89) — fairly pricey at 7 €, but worth every penny if you've had a light meal to start

restaurants
eat

TWO WAYS WITH MUSSELS

Provençal-style *(moules à la provençale)*, pictured

Simplicity itself — especially if you have a serving dish as shown here. Allow 12 small mussels per person. Open them, clean them, and keep

the largest shells. Place the shells in the heatproof serving dish, a mussel in each shell. Mince a bunch of parsely and 4 garlic cloves; mix well and sprinkle over the mussels. (Some recipes call for 1 tbsp breadcrumbs to be added to the parsley mix.) Then pour over olive oil or melted butter and grill for about 5-6min. Serve with lemon wedges — and perhaps pieces of tomato for colour.

<u>Corsican-style: ingre-
dients (for 4 people)</u>

1 kg mussels
2 tomatoes, skinned, de-
seeded and cubed
1 onion, finely sliced
3 garlic cloves
1 bunch parsley, chopped
1 bay leaf
1 sprig of thyme
olive oil
salt and pepper
1 tbsp bread crumbs

Corsican-style *(moules à la mode corse)*, not pictured

Clean the mussels and place them in a heavy casserole with very little water. Heat over a high flame just until they open, then remove and drain. Strain the juice and set aside.

Gently fry the onions, garlic and parsley for 5min. Then add the tomatoes, thyme and bay. Simmer for about 20min. Pour in the reserved liquid; add the mussels and season.

The sauce should be fairly thick; if it is not, add the level tbsp of breadcrumbs. Simmer for another 5min before serving.

'Petit Napoléon'

If you are using dried chestnuts, soak them overnight and cook until tender (about an hour). If using fresh, boil them for a few minutes, skin them, then boil for about another 20 minutes.

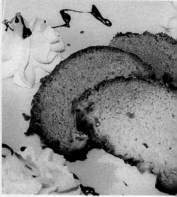

Preheat the oven to 160°C/325°F/gas mark 3. Prepare a loose-bottomed 20 cm/8 in circular cake tin by greasing thoroughly. (At U Furnellu they must use a bread tin, but getting it out may pose a problem!)

Cream the chestnuts in a blender (if you don't have one, mash them very finely with whatever is to hand!). Stir in the apples and walnuts. In a separate container, beat the egg yolks and sugar; add the baking powder and vanilla. Add this mixture to the chestnut purée.

Beat the egg whites until they form soft peaks, then gently fold into the cake mixture.

Cook the cake in the preheated oven for 35min, or until a skewer inserted into the middle comes out clean.

At U Furnellu they serve this cake with whipped cream and some swirls of melted dark chocolate.

Ingredients (for 10 servings)

- 200 g fresh or prepared chestnuts
- 50 g chopped walnuts
- 50 g apples, finely chopped
- 125 g granulated sugar
- 4 eggs, separated
- 1 tsp baking powder
- 1 tsp vanilla

recipes

eat

The Plage de l'Ostriconi lies at the western end of the Sentier du Littoral des Agriates (Walk 9). It's one of the few areas of dunes in Corsica and a textbook habitat for plants and birds. The setting is magnificent: the river meanders through rich farmlands and trees to its mouth at the vivid turquoise sea, collared by white sand dunes.

ostriconi

WALK

Distance: 6km/3.7mi; 1h45min

Grade: easy after a steep, rough descent; be prepared to wade; no shade. IGN map 4249 OT

Equipment: as page 12; sun protection, bathing things, *drinks*

Transport: 🚌 to/from the Plage de l'Ostriconi: the road runs north off the N1197 some 2.5km west of the Ile-Rousse/St-Florent junction to a camp site (Village de l'Ostriconi); park a bit further on, where the road widens out. Or park at the Village restaurant and walk from there

Refreshments: restaurant at the Village de l'Ostriconi (see page 93); *none en route*

Points of interest: dune habitat and the beach

The walk begins at the parking area above the beach. Scramble down the steep path, then wade across the mouth of the Ostriconi River. Cross the Plage de l'Ostriconi and, on the far side, rise up on a track; then fork left on the coastal path. After crossing a streambed, the path runs between two small ruins (i Magazini) and then two old stone pillars (navigational aids). You can end the walk at the Anse de Vana (45min) with a swim, or follow the ongoing path as far as you like.

On your return take the sandy inland track (waymarked with an arrow carved in stone). Pass a signboard for the **Sentier du Littoral (1h10min)**. A few minutes later, at a Y-fork, turn down right to the beach. Walk along the back of the beach until you come to a juniper- and reed-edged creek. Follow the cart track beside it (be prepared to wade) to a little **footbridge** over the **Etang de Foce**. This is an idyllic spot, with eucalyptus and farmland on the far side — and the Village de l'Ostriconi, a lovely place to spend a holiday in the wooden bungalows or campsite.

Return across the beach, and climb to the **car park (1h45min)**. Have a meal at the restaurant at the Village de l'Ostriconi, or, if it's out of season, drive on to l'Ile-Rousse or St-Florent.

VILLAGE DE L'OSTRICONI
2.5km west of the Ile-Rousse/St-Florent junction on the N1197
(04 95 60 10 05
www.village-ostriconi.com
closed from 1/11 till Easter, otherwise open all day €€

full **breakfasts**

large choice of **entrées**, **salads**, **pastas**, **omelettes**, **pizzas** for a light meal.

fish and **seafood**, **steaks**, **veal**, **chicken**

small wine list

Ostriconi

This very attractive restaurant is just as up-market as the 3-star holiday village: one of the sweets was 'chocolate soup with a cinnamon infusion, vanilla-roasted apple slices, and croutons of carmelised spiced bread'! In summer, bar and barbecues on the terrace by the pool.

restaurants

eat

One of the best times to take this delightful ramble is late in the day, when you can sit by the chapel watching the fishing boats, yachts and high-speed ferries making for the port below Calvi's citadel under the setting sun. On the other hand, early mornings are cool (for the climb) and you'll have plenty of time for a swim.

notre-dame de la serra

WALK

The walk starts at the **railway station** in **Calvi**: walk up steps to the main street (Avenue de la République), cross it, and turn left. Now take the first turn to the right (just past the youth hostel). Then take the first left (signpost 'stade'). Turn right in front of the stadium, pass the 'Antenne Medicale' (small hospital) on the right, then go left towards 'Les Aloes'. When the road forks 400m/yds further on, keep left on the road indicated as a cul-de-sac (sign: 'EDF'). Pass a turn to the right and, when your road curls up to the right, watch out for a small sign 'Notre Dame de la Serra' at the right of the entrance to **Villa de Iris** on your left (**15min**).

This sign directs you along a short passage leading to a climb over smooth rock with some steps. You rise to a field, where you can see the chapel,

Distance: 8.5km/5.3mi; 2h10min

Grade: fairly easy ascent/descent of 200m/650ft on good tracks and paths. IGN map 4149 OT

Equipment: as page 12; stout shoes, sun protection, bathing things

Transport: 🚂 to/from Calvi railway station or 🚐 to/from Calvi

Longer walk: la Revellata (15km/9.3mi; 3h40min; grade as main walk, but quite long). Follow the main walk to the Plage de l'Alga (1h30min), then go left on the coastal path. Beyond the largest cove (Anse de l'Oscelluccia), the path rises and eventually climbs to the road to the old lighthouse. Turn right to the lighthouse at the end of the point. From here you can continue 0.5km to the Marine Biology Research Centre: it's private property, but access on foot is allowed. If you would like to visit it, make an appointment in advance (☎ 04 95 65 06 18). Return the same way to the Plage d'Alga and pick up the main walk again.

Refreshments:
bars, cafés, restaurants in Calvi seasonal bar/café at the Plage de l'Alga

Points of interest:
Notre Dame de la Serra; viewpoint la Revellata seascapes

Notre-Dame de la Serra, ahead. Take the clear, *maquis*-lined footpath just to the right of the field. Orange and red waymarks take you all the way to the chapel, **Notre Dame de la Serra (50min)**.

Leave the chapel on the asphalt access road, heading due west (there's little traffic, and 10 minutes down you pass some fascinating skull-like rock formations). When the road forks, keep right and come to the main D81b (**Porto road; 1h10min**).

Turn left here and, almost immediately, turn right on the track to the lighthouse on **la Revellata**. Soon you can take any of the paths or tracks down to the little cove below to the right (green signs, with the welcome word '**bar**', point the way). When you arrive at the beach (**Plage de l'Alga; 1h30min**), indulge in a swim and some refreshment (although the bar may not be open outside high season).

Take the clear footpath from here all the way along the coast back to Calvi. The path ends at a road junction with the entrance to the **Résidences L'Oasis**, on the left. Turn right here. The road, soon

tarred, passes below some wooden holiday bungalows on the right in about five minutes, then leads to the coastal Calvi/Porto road (D81b) by the entrance to the Résidences Tramariccia. Turn left on the main road and follow it past U Fanale (see page 99) and the **citadel**, back to **Calvi station (2h10min)**.

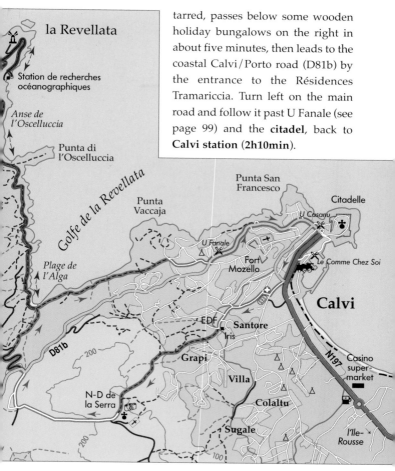

la Revellata

Station de recherches océanographiques

Anse de l'Oscelluccia

Punta di l'Oscelluccia

Golfe de la Revellata

Punta San Francesco

Punta Vaccaja

Citadelle

U Casanu

U Fanale

Fort Mozello

Le Comme Chez Soi

Calvi

Plage de l'Alga

D81b 200

EDF Santore

Iris

Grapi

Villa

N197

Casino super-market

l'Ile-Rousse

N-D de la Serra

Colaltu

Sugale

200

100

La Revellata: the Marine Biology Research Centre and old lighthouse

U Fanale

This restaurant, just 150m the Calvi side of where the walk comes back to the Porto road after the Résidences Tramariccia, is named for its view to the setting opposite — the Revellata lighthouse (*fanale*).

Our first impression was that the menu was pretentious and the à la carte dishes quite expensive, but there are two very economical 'menus' — one at 16 € and a 'Menu Corse' at 23 €. If you are just after a light meal, the pizzas range from only 6 € to 9.80 €.

The presentation of the food matches the menu: their risotto with crayfish is shown on page 104 — truly a work of art, *and* it was superb. Our only complaint was that the food was not piping hot: *no* restaurants on Corsica seem to warm plates, and at U Fanale everything is *carried by hand* up from the downstairs kitchen!

U FANALE
Route de Porto, Calvi
(04 95 65 18 82
daily from May until 31 Oct, then Thu-Sat evenings only, Sun lunch and dinner €-€€€

7 **entrées**: *salade du pêcheur* (giant prawns, crayfish, scallops), terrine of salmon and swordfish, tart of Corsican *coppa* (see page 8), Corsican charcuterie, 'melt' of warm goats' cheese *(chevre)*, fish soup, Corsican soup (recipe page 102)

pastas include salmon in tagliatelli or with pan-fried giant prawns

fish: locally-caught swordfish with a little tomato and thyme tart and sweet pepper chutney; daurade in a mille-feuille pastry, risotto with crayfish (recipe page 104)

wide range of **omelettes**

meats: rumpsteak with cognac and mushroom sauce; lamb in a crispyskin with rosemary-flavoured olives and a sweet garlic cream; duck breast with fritters *(beignets)*, figs and *foie gras*; veal escalope in cream sauce

sweets: *fiadone* (recipe page 123); fruit with Corsican muscat wine; crème brulée; *mi-cuit au chocolat noir* (individual puddings made with dark chocolate, sugar, eggs, butter and a bit of flour); milk pudding with licorice and cream flavoured with green tea

U Casanu

If you're not 'in the know', and you make straight for the port, you may walk past this *minuscule* restaurant without even seeing it. But once you've eaten there, you'll return again and again,

Leg of lamb on a sizzle platter

U CASANU
18 Boulevard Wilson, Calvi
(04 95 65 00 10
closed 1/11-15/12 and Sun €€

a **speciality** is leg of lamb, first cooked for 7 hours, then sizzled when presented and served with a 'ratatouille' of roasted vegetables, all in a sweet-sour sauce

also **authentic Corsican food**: *suppa corse* (recipe overleaf), *figatellu* (pork liver sausage) with eggs, fantastic *al dente* pastas, Corsican charcuterie, *bouillabaisse* with sardines and saffron, local fish and seafood, duck, an unusual cassoulet, *stuffatu* (recipe page 103), *carpaccio* of salmon

Orsini **wines** (the vineyard on the road to Calenzana)

until you have worked your way through the menu!

Despite the very pretty, pale green French country-style décor, the chef, Omae Hiromassa, is Japanese! But the Japanese influence is only apparent in some dishes, like this lamb sizzle-platter; others are 100 per cent Corsican, perfectly cooked.

Mme Luciani, the owner, is a tremendously welcoming hostess and has been running this treasure for over 10 years.

restaurants

eat

Le Comme Chez Soi

Most people make for the marina-side restaurants and cafés, where the most widely-publicised restaurant is U Calellu. They must

LE COMME CHEZ SOI
Quai Landry (04 95 65 45 81
closed 15/11-10/2 and Wed in low
season €€-€€€

specialities are fish and seafood, but there are meat dishes as well

8 **entrées**, from the usual plate of Corsican meats and fish soup to *foie gras* with crayfish and an aspic of Corsican Muscatel wine

fish and seafood of all kinds in varied sauces, grilled, fried or poached (nb: *some* of the fish dishes are charged by *weight*)

meats include duck with raspberries, Corsican lamb, wild boar in chestnut honey, fillet steak in a reduced wine sauce

'menu gourmand' at only 20 €, with a choice of 4 entrées, 4 mains and 3 sweets

'menu des fins gourmets' at 48 € – this includes a lobster main course

good selection of Corsican **wines**

Daurade in shellfish sauce

do well, as they were already closed for the season by mid-October! Some of the other restaurants had limited or 'boring' menus, but Le Comme Chez Soi caters for a very wide range of tastes and budgets.

We started with Corsican-style mussels (recipe page 88) and, when it came to the 'fish of the day', we were offered a choice of five fish landed that day in addition to those on the menu. Of course, one of the pleasures of eating here is being part of the lively marina-side atmosphere, from the first apéritif to the post-prandial coffee and brandy!

Traditional Corsican soup *(suppa corsa)*

Soak the beans overnight (or cheat and use tinned!). Cut the cabbage into wedges and the potatoes into large cubes. Slice the carrots thickly and quarter the tomatoes. Mince the chard, onions and garlic.

Heat the oil in a large, deep heavy-bottomed saucepan and cook the vegetables for about 3min, untill golden. Then pour over the water, add the beans and put in the ham bone. *(If you are using tinned beans, add them just 10min before cooking finishes.)*

Bring to the boil, then turn down and leave it to just lightly bubble for about 2h, skimming when necessary. Season halfway through the cooking, remembering that the ham is already salty!

About 10min before the vegetables are cooked, add the beans if tinned, and macaroni. The latter is optional (some recipes call for stale bread instead), but remember, this is intended to be a *very* thick soup. Stir in the minced herbs at the last minute.

Ingredients (for 4 people)

1 bone of dry Corsican (or similar) ham, with some meat
1/2 small cabbage
250 g Swiss chard (or pak choi)
3 waxy potatoes
1 carrot
2 onions
2 tomatoes
200 g dry haricot beans
150g macaroni
2 garlic cloves, crushed
2 tbsp olive oil
2 l water
salt and pepper
fresh basil and marjoram, minced

recipes

eat

Meat stew with smoked ham *(stuffatu)*

If you are using dry mushrooms, soak them in some warm water (for about 30min). Cut all the meat into cubes, dice the ham, mince the onions and crush the garlic.

In a heavy-bottomed casserole, fry all the above (except the mushrooms) in olive oil for about 10min, turning to brown all sides. Pour in the wine, and stir in the tomato paste. Add the mushrooms, bouquet garni, and salt and pepper to taste.

Bring everything to the boil, then lower the heat and cook on top of the hob for about 2h30min-3h, until the meat is meltingly tender.

On Corsica, of course this stew is served with pasta (usually tagliatelli), but it is equally good with mashed or boiled potatoes.

Ingredients (for 4 people)

400 g beef (shoulder)
400 g lamb (shoulder)
250 g *prizuttu* (prosciutto), sliced fairly thick
400 g fresh ceps (porcini mushrooms), or 100 g dry mushrooms
2 onions
3 cloves of garlic
0.5 l red wine
1 bouquet garni
1 level tbsp tomato paste
olive oil
salt and pepper

The ubiquitous *salade bergère* (shown below at La Cave, l'Ile-Rousse) pops up on all menus. Easy to make at home, it contains grilled cheese *(brocciu* or *chevre)* on bread, Corsican ham(s), tomatoes, pickles, and other ingredients to taste — perhaps peppers, cucumber, raw mushrooms, raisins, pine nuts, walnuts, black olives, figs or fig chuttney. All served on a bed of *very fresh* lettuce, in a vinaigrette sweetened with a delicate Corsican honey rather than sugar.

103

Langoustine risotto
(risotto aux langoustines)

Well, we are not going to show you our version of this dish when we can show you U Fanale's for inspiration! It tasted as good as it looked. If Dublin Bay prawns elude you, use readily-available tiger prawns.

In a medium heavy skillet, gently fry the onions and peppers in some oil for a few minutes, until golden. Pour in the wine and leave to simmer on the lowest heat. Just a few minutes before the rice (see below) has finished cooking, put the prawns, including the four in their shells (used later to decorate), into this wine mixture and heat through.

Meanwhile, warm 2 tbsp of oil in a large heavy-bottomed skillet. Add the rice and stir constantly for a couple of minutes. Then add the stock a little at a time, always stirring, until all the liquid is taken up and the rice is tender and creamy (about 20min).

Gently stir in the prawn and wine mixture and decorate quickly, to serve piping hot!

Ingredients (for 4 people)

350 g arborio rice
350 g cooked, shelled *langoustines* (Dublin Bay prawns), cut into bite-sized pieces
4 whole *langoustines,* unshelled
600 ml fish stock
150 ml dry white wine
4 spring onions, sliced (including the green tops)
1/2 green pepper, diced
1/2 red pepper, diced
salad greens, like *mesclun*
2 lemons
3-4 tbsp olive oil
salt and pepper
optional: grapes, flowers and pastry fantasies to decorate!

recipes

eat

Pork and chestnut terrine (terrine de porc aux châtaignes)

Put the minced shallot in a dish and just cover with oil; set aside. Take 5 outside cabbage leaves and boil them in salted water for 1min; drain, *dry* and set aside. Finely chop the rest of the cabbage (about 400 g), cook for 10min, then drain, *dry* and set aside.

Fry the pork loins in a little oil just to stiffen and shrink them (or they will shrink too much in the terrine). In a bowl, mix the pork mince, chopped cabbage, shallot, chestnuts, myrtle leaves, cognac, eggs and salt and pepper to taste. *Quickly fry a small ball of this mixture to check the seasoning!*

Preheat the oven to 180°C/350°F/gas mark 4. Line a 2 l earthenware terrine (it must have a lid with a hole) with the bacon strips, then press in a layer of cabbage leaves. Press in half the mixture, *hard* (it will shrink in cooking). Put in a layer of the pork loin, trimmed to fit so that it does not overlap. Cover with the rest of the mixture, top with cabbage leaves and bacon strips. Cover.

Put the terrine in a bain-marie or roasting tin with boiling water and cook for about 2h30min-3h, making sure there is always enough *simmering* water. It will be done when a skewer inserted into the centre *for a full half minute* comes out hot! Cool at room temperature before serving.

Ingredients (8-16 servings)

- 600 g pork shoulder, roughly minced
- 3 pork loins, deboned, fat trimmed off, pounded to about 1 cm thickness
- 600 g green cabbage
- 300 g prepared chestnuts, whole
- 1 shallot, minced
- 4 medium eggs, beaten
- 10 wild myrtle leaves
- 1 shot glass cognac
- salt and pepper
- a little sunflower oil
- 250 g finely sliced *panzetta* (to line the terrine)

Discover the enchanting villages of the Balagne on foot. This 'starter' walk can be done in either direction (perhaps depending on which restaurant you fancy), or as a very short circuit. But by using the notes and maps for Walk 13, you *could* do a 21km-long 'grand tour' — from Lumio to l'Ile-Rousse.

lumio, occi & lavatoggio

WALK

From Lavatoggio to Lumio:
Start the walk at the D71 in
Lavatoggio. Climb the steps
just west of the **church** (faded
orange waymark). At the top,
turn right on **Allée Roger
Dassonville** (sign on the right:
'**Lumio 1h25min**'). You look
back across the valley to the
square church tower at
Aregno and to Sant' Antonino
straddling a hill. Continue up
the concrete lane to a tiny
chapel, **San Giovanni di
Venti** (15min).

Now follow the cart track
at the left of the chapel, until
you come to another little
chapel, **Notre Dame de la
Stella** (45min). From here the
main trail goes straight ahead
to Lumio. But to first visit
Occi, turn right on a cart track
some 10m east of the chapel
(orange paint waymarks).
Follow the waymarks care-
fully, eventually bearing left
and rising through white

Distance: 7km/4.3mi; 2h-2h20min
one way

Grade: quite easy, especially in the
direction Lavatoggio to Lumio (overall
ascent 150m/490ft); from Lumio to
Lavatoggio ascent of 255m/835ft.
Good tracks and paths throughout;
waymarking varies: *keep alert! No
shade.* IGN maps 4149 OT, 4249 OT

Equipment: as page 12; take a
sunhat and plenty of water

Transport: 🚗 car to/from Lavatoggio or Lumio, in which case you
will have to *walk both ways.* The
easiest alternative is to leave your car
at Lumio, take a taxi to Lavatoggio,
and walk back to Lumio (easier
gradients).

Alternative walk: Occi circuit
(5.5km/3.4mi; 2h; moderate ascent/
descent of 255m/835ft). 🚗 to/from
the north entrance to Lumio on the
N197. Park just inside the road,
opposite the Hotel Chez Charles. See
notes on page 110.

Refreshments:
Chez Charles at Lumio, Chez Edgard
(dinner only!) and a not-always-open
café at Lavatoggio; *none en route*

Points of interest:
ruined village of Occi
views over the coast

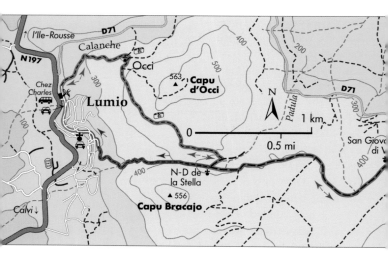

cistus. When the climb levels out (**1h05min**), you have a fine view to Calvi, la Revellata, the Bonifatu mountains, and Capu d'Occi up to the right. Ignore a path up to the right; keep ahead downhill — to the dramatically perched ruins of **Occi** (**1h20min**).

From the **church**, with the **building dated 1785** on your left, walk towards a stone wall and then left, away from Occi. Ignore a good path on the right with a faded red waymark (it descends to the 'Panoramic' camp site on the D71). Circling Occi, wait until the lighthouse at la Revellata comes into view, then descend an old stone-laid mule trail (more orange waymarks). You zigzag down through pink boulders (the '**Calanche**'). Go through a gap in a fence and, on coming to a three-way fork,

The ruins of Occi

take either track to the right, passing a colourfully-planted house on the left. The waymarks lead you to a lane behind the Hotel Chez Charles: pick up your car at the nearby car park, or fork left uphill into **Lumio** (**2h**).

From Lumio to Lavatoggio: **Start out** at **Chez Charles**: take the lane behind the hotel (sign: '**Village d'Occi**'). Orange waymarks mark the old mule trail to the ruined village of **Occi** (**45min**). From Occi follow a path which ascends southeast (more orange waymarks and some cairns). You rise through white cistus, then descend to a crossing trail and the little chapel of **Notre-Dame de la Stella** (**1h25min**). At the chapel, turn left on a cart track and follow this to another tiny chapel, **San Giovanni di Venti**

109

At the Calanche

(**2h05min**). Now keep straight ahead along a concrete lane (**Allée Roger Dassonville**); this takes you down to the **church** at **Lavatoggio** (**2h20min**).

Lumio — Occi — Lumio circuit: **Start out** at **Chez Charles**: follow the notes for the Lumio to Lavatoggio route all the way to the chapel of **Notre-Dame de la Stella** (**1h25min**). Turn right here and just keep straight on (due west), to descend quite steeply back to **Lumio** (**2h**).

Chez Charles and Chez Edgard

There are good restaurants at both ends of this walk, and they are very different. **Chez Charles** is an upmarket hotel with an elegant dining room and a gorgeous terrace for dining in summer. Just click on 'restaurant' on their web site, then click on *'voir photos des plats'* to see what you're paying for!

Whereas you *could* have a fairly light, à la carte meal at Chez Charles, be prepared to take a hearty appetite to **Chez Edgard** in Lavatoggio! This is an informal *ferme-auberge*, a working farm

CHEZ CHARLES
N 197, Lumio (04 95 60 61 71
www.hotel-chezcharles.com
closed Nov-Mar €€-€€€
specialities: wide range of fish dishes; veal, duck, pork cheek
seasonal menu at 32 €
'plaisir' menu at 40 €

CHEZ EDGARD
D71, Lavatoggio (04 95 61 70 75
dinner only, and only by reservation, Easter to Oct €€
specialities: skewered meat cooked on an open fire – sometimes duck, sometimes lamb, suckling pig (if ordered in advance), veal sautéed with figs and prunes, wild boar (in the hunting season), Corsican soup, *brocciu* fritters, tart with Corsican herbs, chestnut cake
menu 32 €

offering meals of traditional regional dishes. The menu is thus limited and meat-based, but you will enjoy some of the best cooking on Corsica: all the food has been raised or cultivated by the family, members of a proud local farming tradition.

Both restaurants are long-established.

restaurants

eat

Chez Charles gives a recipe on their web site for a 'minimalist' lobster appetizer with citrus dressing. We've adapted it to make a refreshing luncheon salad.

Seafood salad with a citrus vinaigrette
(salade de fruits de mer en vinaigrette d'agrumes)

First make the vinaigrette by mixing all the ingredients except the garlic and onions in a jar with a lid; shake well to mix, and set aside. *Just before serving,* add the garlic and onions and shake again to mix; pour into a serving dish.

At Chez Charles the presentation is spartan and artistic; the only greenery being a few sprigs of rocket. But for a heartier lunch, we opt for the very freshest butterhead lettuce (round lettuce hearts) as a base — while keeping the rocket decoration.

As for the seafood, we like about 500 g of tiger prawns, 250 g fresh crab meat and 250 g lobster. Cold scallops are equally delicious.

A dry white or rosé wine and some crusty bread makes a feast of this meal.

<u>Ingredients (for 4 people)</u>
1 kg mixed cooked seafood
200 g cherry tomatoes
2 basil leaves, torn up
salad greens to taste
<u>for the vinaigrette</u>:
1 tbsp lemon juice
1 tbsp grapefruit juice

2 tbsp orange juice
100 g purée of ripe mangoes
4 tbsp olive oil
salt and pepper
5 g chopped peeled garlic
15 g finely sliced spring onions

Veal sauté with prunes and figs (sauté de veau aux pruneaux et figues)

Our version of this Chez Edgard dish is easily cooked on the hob.

In a heavy-bottomed skillet (for which you have a lid), fry the bacon bits, onions and garlic in oil until golden and set aside. Then brown the veal in hot oil on all sides and set aside.

Mix 1 tbsp oil and 1 tbsp flour to a paste. Pour some stock into the skillet and heat gently, scraping up any flavourful bits. Add the oil/flour paste, stirring all the time, so that it doesn't form lumps. Add the rest of the stock, the wine, and the tomato paste, still stirring. Bring to the boil and add the herbs and spices, dried figs and prunes. Season.

Return the reserved ingredients to the skillet, cover and cook slowly for 1 hour or so, until the meat is tender and the sauce has reduced. Just before serving, you may wish to stir in a shot glass of cognac and flame it.

Ingredients (for 4 people)

800 g veal shoulder, rib or tenderloin, cut into large cubes
50 g unsmoked bacon bits
1 large onion, chopped
2 cloves garlic, crushed
200 ml veal (or chicken) stock
200 ml dry white wine
50-100 g each dried figs and prunes, quartered (to taste)
1 tbsp tomato paste
sprig of thyme; 1 bay leaf
2 sprigs of flat parsley
1 level tbsp Corsican herbs
5 juniper berries, crushed
olive oil for frying
1 tbsp flour
salt and pepper

recipes

eat

Together with Walk 12, this short downhill ramble from Sant' Antonino — the most beautiful village in the Balagne — to bustling l'Ile-Rousse, gives you a good overview of the area. But if the weather is cool and breezy, then we heartily recommend the Alternative walk — it's a 'grand tour' in every sense, a really magnificent hike!

sant' antonino & l'île-rousse

WALK

The walk starts in **Sant' Antonino**, at the village **car park**. But before setting out, be sure to explore the beautiful village and fortify yourself with some lip-puckering freshly-squeezed *lemon* juice at the Cave à Citron (see page 121)!

Then take the dirt track 100m to the left of the **church**, heading for a **cemetery** on a rise. At a fork about 200m/yds along, go *right* (the fork to the left *may* be signposted to the Couvent de Corbara). This sandy track is *not* signposted, but it affords better views and avoids an unnecessary climb in full sun from Corbara. You rise over a **pass** and pass a track up to the relay station on **Capu Corbinu** (**15min**). This is a brilliant viewpoint down over Pigna and Corbara, with the Couvent de Corbara in the foreground, backed by the Cima Sant' Angelo.

Distance: 8km/5mi; 2h10min

Grade: easy descent of 450m/1475ft on good tracks and paths. The waymarks are faint and infrequent, but the route is straightforward. *IGN maps 4149 OT, 4249 OT*

Equipment: as page 12; sunhat!

Transport: 🚗 taxi or with friends to Sant' Antonino; return by 🚌 from l'Île-Rousse (see page 133)

Alternative walk: la Balagne (21km/13mi; 6h; moderate, but long. *Almost no shade.* Overall ascent: 550m/1800ft; descent 650m/2130ft). Follow Walk 12 *from Lumio to Lavatoggio* (page 109). Then use the map and *carefully* follow waymarking, remembering that you should always be on a *good* path (the remains of an old mule trail). Leaving Lavatoggio, be sure not to descend too far; the path is only 25m/80ft below the D71. Turn left at the cemetery just before Cateri: the trail continues from below the Hotel San Dume. Go through Aregno to the Pisan Romanesque Eglise de la Trinité (12C), then climb to Sant' Antonino. Now pick up Walk 13.

Refreshments: cafés, bars, restaurants in Sant' Antonino and l'Île-Rousse (see page 121); *none en route*

Points of interest: Sant' Antonino and l'Île-Rousse — and the views!

At a T-junction, keep left downhill (**25min**). Two minutes later you come to a barrage of signposts on the left. The path from the Couvent de Corbara comes in here from the left. Keep *right* (you may spot the odd orange flash). As you pass below the **Cima Sant' Angelo** (see map overleaf) you have a good view down to l'Ile-Rousse and its light-house; in the middle distance, cypresses and a slender church tower announce Occiglioni, the next village en route.

Approaching Occiglione

You soon pass a beautiful old **ruined convent** on the right (**40min**). Palmento is the village just below to the east. Be sure to take a break under the venerable oak here — the only shade for miles around! Then follow the track into an S-bend. You'll be surprised when you see that you have *passed* Occiglioni's church! Don't worry, your turn-off back to the village is just ahead: as the track curves left,

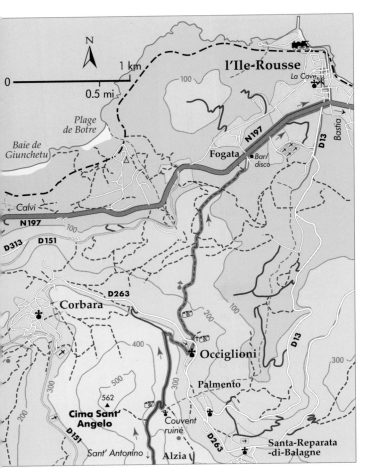

Descending to l'Île-Rousse

watch for your narrow path down to the right (**50min**; there may be a cairn). Orange flashes eventually guide you down into **Occiglioni** (**55min**), which you enter on a cobbled lane. Walk to the left of the **church** and then follow the cobbles downhill under an arch. Go straight ahead between the houses and in two minutes you come to the D263, by a **viewpoint with an iron cross**.

Go down the concrete steps just to the left of the viewpoint (orange flash). At a Y-fork immediately, keep left. From up here you enjoy good views of your final destination. You pass a

The plane-shaded square in l'Ile-Rousse is the perfect spot for a break — or have a meal at La Cave, next to the church.

lovely old **fountain** on the left (**1h 10min**); cobbles underfoot remind you that you're on what was once a beautiful old mule trail; sadly, it is now mostly sand or rubble. Seven or eight minutes later, a stream merges with the path, and the going may be a bit wet underfoot.

You've lost the views of l'Ile-Rousse by now. At a fork, go straight ahead (**1h22min**; signpost '**Ile-Rousse**'). The sign says that l'Ile-Rousse is just 15 minutes away — but the station is still *50 minutes* away. Continue through the *maquis*, pungent with the odour of yellow-flowering Jerusalem sage. Cross over a track to a house on the left and rejoin the path. Two minutes later, go straight across a sandy cross-path. In another 10 minutes, at a complicated intersection, just go straight ahead on bedrock. Six minutes later you pass a house on the left with a very pretty fountain. On reaching a tarred lane two minutes later, turn left, down to the main N197, by a **bar/disco** (**1h45min**). Turn right to l'Ile-Rousse; after enjoying some refreshments or a meal, walk on to the **railway station** by the port (**2h10min**).

Cave à Citron and La Cave

You're spoilt for choice: there are at least five or six restaurants in Sant' Antonino (but most are closed between October and Easter). We usually start the day by visiting the **Cave à Citron** (open from Easter to 30 Oct) — the large yellow building opposite the car park. This very popular establishment, a village landmark, not only sells lemon juice (you add your own sugar to taste), but almonds (a tonne each year), honey, jams, olive oil and muscat wines (from the Antonini family's neighbouring vineyards). The spotless winery is in a nearby garage.

The Antonini winery

We'll then have lunch at **La Cave** in l'Ile-Rousse — a delightful restaurant next to the church, with a pretty outdoor terrace. Their menu is just amazing — not only for the huge choice, but the low prices. You can have fish or meat grilled over a wood fire — or pan-fried with an endless variety of sauces. As with most of our chosen restaurants, it is family-run, so they know the ingredients of all their dishes. Their home-made chestnut cake is 100% chestnut flour; we always buy extra slices of this *and* the *fiadone,* to take home!

> **LA CAVE**
> **Place Paoli (next to the church),**
> **l'Ile-Rousse** (**04 95 60 33 41**
> **closed Jan and Mon in winter €-€€**
> **menus at 11.50 €, 14.50 €, 7 € (kids)**
>
> **huge à la carte menu:** far too many dishes to list; virtually whatever you want, from 6 kinds of **pizzas**, **omelettes**, 14 **salads**, over a dozen different **fish/seafood** plates, **meats** of all kinds, home-made **desserts**
>
> the **menu corse at 13 €** offers three courses: 6 choices of entrée, 6 choices of main course and either *fiadone and* chestnut cake or cheeses

restaurants

eat

Corsican-style red mullet (rougets à la mode corse)

John declared these the best *rougets* ever. Luckily we visited La Cave out of season, so we had time to ask the owner endless questions about ingredients. Although we don't know all the details of preparation, our version of this very quick and easy dish is a pretty fair match.

In a small saucepan, gently fry the garlic cloves until they are translucent. Pour over the bisque and tinned tomatoes and bring just to the boil, then immediately turn down the heat and leave to simmer while the fish are cooking. We usually add some Corsican herbs at this stage, but that is only because we seem to add them to *everything*; it's optional.

Tiny red mullet fry up very quickly, and most French recipes call for them to be fried, *unfloured*, on one side only — the skin side. Since you probably can't deal with all 12 at once, keep a plate warm in the oven to receive them. Cook for just 2-3min, just until the flesh changes colour.

Just before serving, tear the basil leaves into pieces and stir them into the sauce.

Ingredients (for 4 people)

12 small red mullets (*rougets*), filletted
100 g tinned tomatoes
1 tin (300 g) lobster bisque
2 garlic cloves, crushed
8 basil leaves
1 tbsp Corsican herbs (optional)
1 tbsp olive oil

recipes

eat

Our photograph shows the chestnut cake (left) at La Cave and their *fiadone*. We've only given the recipe for the *fiadone* but, if you want to make a truly delicious, pure chestnut cake, then use the recipe on page 89, but *instead of the apples and walnuts*, just use 300 g of prepared chestnuts. Preparation method is the same; cooking time will be about 35min.

Fiadone (pictured right)

Preheat the oven to 180°C/350°F/gas mark 4. Beat the eggs and sugar together until fluffy. Crush the *brocciu* with a fork into very fine bits and beat into the egg/sugar mixture with the lemon zest.

Pour into a lined and well-greased, fairly deep 25 cm/9 in pie tin with a removable bottom and bake for 45min, or until a knife inserted into middle comes out clean. As you can see, this is 'cake' does not rise much — it will only be about 2.5 cm high. Let the cake cool in the oven, to avoid the top cracking or caving in.

Tip: To make a lighter *fiadone*, separate the eggs and beat the whites before mixing with the yolks and sugar.

Ingredients (12-16 servings)
500 g *brocciu frais* (or ricotta)
300 g caster sugar
6 eggs
grated rind of one lemon

A train journey into Corsica's interior is a must. Our suggestions — travelling north or travelling south — do not cover the whole route. Instead we take in the most spectacular stretch, allowing you to combine the trip with a short walk and an enjoyable lunch.

'u trinichellu'

EXCURSION

The Corsicans affectionately use the diminutive 'little train' ('U Trinichellu') when referring to their narrow-gauge railway ... although TGV (Train à Grandes *Vibrations*) is now gaining currency! Tiny it may be, with just two cars, but it is famous round the world.

Like all mountain railways, this was a very difficult project, involving 32 tunnels (one of them 4km long) and 76 bridges and viaducts (including the 140m-long viaduct above the Vecchio River). There used to be another, busy line serving Porto-Vecchio, but it was destroyed by bombing during World War II and never rebuilt.

Rather than describe the route in detail, we highlight and comment briefly on the landmarks in both directions. This is a wonderful day out: you will glide past verdant pastures, meander into side-

Our suggestions: travel north from Ajaccio as far as Corte, or south from Ponte Leccia as far as Vizzavona.

Timings and logistics:
Depart Ajaccio 08.25; arrive at Corte 10.47. Stroll up the Restonica road, have lunch, and then look around Corte in the afternoon. Depart Corte 17.15; arrive Ajaccio 19.30.
Depart Ponte Leccia 10.11; arrive at Vizzavona 11.39. Walk from the station via the Cascades des Anglais to the Hotel Monte d'Oro for lunch, then return the same way for the train at 16.21; arrive Ponte Leccia 17.52.

Web site: ter-sncf-com

Station telephone numbers (recheck times in advance!):
Ajaccio (04 95 23 11 03
Bastia (04 95 32 80 61
Calvi (04 95 65 00 61
l'Ile-Rousse (04 95 60 00 50
Ponte Leccia (04 95 46 00 97

Lunch suggestions:
Auberge de la Restonica (a 2km walk from Corte)
Hotel Monte d'Oro (a 4km walk from Vizzavona)

Points of interest:
splendid scenery throughout
Vecchio Viaduct

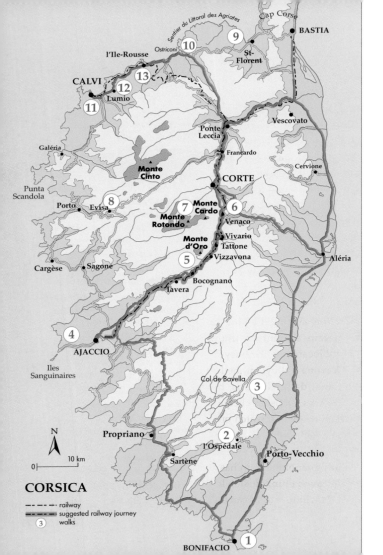

valleys with views to gorges and waterfalls or around promontories at the edge of spectacular cliffs, groan your way up or down through tunnels and overhanging forests of laricio pine, beech and oak. You will see much of the most beautiful scenery of inland Corsica, with mountains

You can pick up your Ponte Leccia connection by taking the Calvi line. Here's the station at l'Ile-Rousse, with a modern diesel and one of the old cars in the background.

rising to over 2600 metres, at the heart of the Regional Natural Park.

Travelling north (sit on the left for the best views):
- **Ajaccio station:** an impressive 19th-century station in a vibrant location at the busy port;
- **Gravona Valley:** on the far side of the river and the N193 is the **Canal de la Gravona**, built to bring water to Ajaccio; it's history was almost as chequered as the railway's;
- leaving **Tavera**, watch on the *right* for a waterfall called the 'Bridal Veil' (**Voile de la Mariée**), at its best in winter and spring;
- **Bocognano:** the train has already climbed over 600m;
- **Vizzavona tunnel:** 4km long — and so straight that from the driver's window light can be seen at the far end;

- **Vizzavona:** at 906m, the highest point of the line, at the foot of **Monte d'Oro** (2389m); crossroads of the **GR20**; also the **Cascades des Anglais** (Walk 5);
- **Tattone**: another fine walking centre, but the train only stops here on request;
- approaching and leaving **Vivario** the train makes two **deep U-bends** where the engineers were unable to pierce tunnels; this is one of the steepest parts of the line; watch for the N193 and the lower stretch of the railway line far below;
- **Vecchio Viaduct:** engineered by Gustav Eiffel; 140m long and 96m high — probably the most exciting part of the route. It's been said that tour operators were keen to make the viaduct a bungee-jumping site;
- **Venaco**, at the centre of the island (and the Regional Natural Park, founded in 1972); many large houses built by wealthy families in the 19th century;
- **Poggio-Riventosa:** like Tattone, this is a request stop and another fine walking base (see our Walk 6)
- **Corte:** at the confluence of the Tavignano and Restonica gorges, historical capital of the island, university founded by Pasquale Paoli, citadel, access to our Walk 7.

Travelling south (sit on the right for the best views):
Why, you might wonder, do we start the northbound route at Ponte Leccia? It's just to allow you to stay in bed a little longer, since by car you'll reach Ponte Leccia in less time than the train. But you can, if you prefer, catch this same train by starting from Calvi at 8.20, Ile-Rousse at 8.53 or Bastia at 9.05.

- **Ponte Leccia:** the only junction on the line, with two separate tracks (where the line from Calvi comes in);
- **Golo River** (Corsica's most important watercourse) is on the *left,* but crossed just after **Francardo,** with a fine view up the Golo Valley to **Monte Cinto** (2706m) on the *right.*
- **Col San Quilico:** some 350m above Ponte Leccia;
- then see notes opposite, as you reach **Corte,** then **Poggio-Riventosa, Venaco,** the **Vecchio Viaduct, Vivario,** Tat-**tone** and **Vizzavona.**

Not a cow or goat on the line, but a penned-in donkey at Tattone. Animals are free to stray onto the tracks, causing delays. Unfortunately they are often killed or have to be put down.

Here are two *panzetta* (Corsican streaky bacon) recipes we've picked up on the island and made at home with great success. Neither is illustrated.

Braised endives with *panzetta* (*endives braisées à la panzetta*)

Braise the endives in a skillet with the water, sugar, butter, thyme, salt and pepper. Reduce until the endives are slightly caramelised (about 30min), then add the vinegar. Grill the *panzetta* for about 2min on one side, then place it, ungrilled side up, above the endives and grill the lot, still in the skillet, for another 3min.

Beans Corsican-style (*haricots à la mode corse*)

Again, we make a cheat's version, by using tinned beans. Preheat the oven to 180°C/350°F/gas mark 4.

In a heavy casserole fry together the onions, *panzetta*, carrots and garlic for 5min, stirring constantly. Then add the tomatoes, the beans (haricot or butter beans are equally good) and the bouquet garni, and just cover with cold water. Season and stir together.

Cover the the casserole and cook for 30min. Remove the bouquet garni before serving.

These beans are lovely with grilled sausages!

For the endives: ingredients (for 4 people)

8 endives
8 thin slices of
    panzetta
125 g butter
300 ml water
50 g caster sugar
2 tbsp balsamic vinegar
salt and pepper
sprig of thyme

For the beans: ingredients (for 4 people)

400 g tinned haricot or
    butter beans
100 g *panzetta*, in
    small cubes
2 tomatoes, peeled, de-
    seeded and chopped
2 onions, minced
2 carrots, sliced
2 cloves garlic, chopped
1 bouquet garni
olive oil

recipes

eat

Chestnut sauerkraut with chestnut beer
(*choucroute aux châtaignes à la bière Pietra*)

You will need a large, shallow, heavy casserole (diametre about 35 cm/14 in), otherwise divide all the ingredients between two smaller ones (as in the photograph, a casserole for 2-3 people). Preheat the oven to 190°C/375°F/gas mark 5.

Sweat the carrots in a little oil, then drain and set aside. In the same skillet, sweat the minced onion. Mix the onion and chestnuts into the sauerkraut.

Wrap the bay leaves and peppercorns in a little muslin, to make a bouquet garni.

Line the bottom of the casserole with 200 g pork belly slices. Cover with the sauerkraut mixture, and tuck in the muslin bag of bay leaves and peppercorns and the bouquet garni.

Arrange the rest of the pork belly and the carrots on top. Pour over the beer and, if all the ingredients are not covered, add water — or more beer. Bring to the boil on the hob, then place in the oven. It will take a good two hours to cook through.

Remove the bouquet garni, bay and peppercorns. Serve with boiled potatoes, dark country bread and chestnut beer! Or, for a 'meatier' meal, use this dish as an accompaniment to pork, ham or sausages.

Ingredients (for 4 people)
- 600 g bottled sauerkraut, drained)
- 1 onion, peeled and minced
- 200 g prepared chestnuts
- 3 carrots, halved lengthwise
- 1 bouquet garni
- 10 bay leaves
- 10 black peppercorns
- 300 g sliced smoked pork belly
- 500 ml Pietra (chestnut) beer
- 4 tbsp sunflower oil

Public transport: bus and train

Walk 1: a) 🚌 Ajaccio—Bonifacio (Eurocorse Voyages, (04 95 21 06 30). Year-round departures Mon-Sat (also Sun/holidays between 1/7-15/9) from the bus station at Ajaccio's port. Departs Ajaccio 08.30, Propriano 10.15, Porto Vecchio 12.00; arrives Bonifacio 12.30. Departs Bonifacio 14.00; arrives Ajaccio 18.00. **b)** 🚌 Porto-Vecchio—Bonifacio (same operator, (04 95 70 13 83). Departs Mon-Sat from rue Pasteur 08.00, 13.00*, 15.00*; arrives Bonifacio 30min later. Departs Bonifacio 16.15*, 19.00. (*only 15/9-6/7)

Walk 2: no public transport, but the Bavella service (see Walk 3) could be used, alighting at l'Ospédale (from where strong walkers could follow the Mare a Mare Sud). Otherwise, ask if you can alight at the turn-off for Cartalavonu, then walk to the nature trail (see page 27).

Walk 3: 🚌 Porto-Vecchio—Bavella (Autocars Balesi, (04 95 51 25 56). Year-round departures Mon-Fri (also Sat in Jul/Aug). Departs Porto-Vecchio 07.00, l'Ospédale 07.20; arrives Bavella 08.15. Departs Bavella 18.05, l'Ospédale 18.45; arrives Porto-Vecchio 19.15.

Walk 4: 🚌 Ajaccio—La Parata (city bus No 5). Daily departures from the Place Général de Gaulle; journey time 20min. (Note that from 1/7 to 31/8 services are more frequent; from 1/11 to 31/3 they may be less frequent.) Departs Ajaccio 07.05, 08.05, 09.05, 10.05, 11.05, 12.05, 13.05, 14.05, 17.05, 18.05, 19.05; departs La Parata 07.30, 08.30, 09.30, 10.30, 11.30, 12.30, 13.30, 14.30, 17.30, 18.30, 19.30

Walk 5: a) 🚌 service Ajaccio—Bastia (Eurocorse Voyages, (04 95 21 06 31). Departures Mon-Sat only from the bus station at Ajaccio's port and from 1, rue du Nouveau Port in Bastia

Ajaccio	Vizzavona	Vivario	Venaco	Corte	P. Leccia	Bastia
07.45	08.40	08.55	09.05	09.30	09.55	10.45

TRANSPORT

Bastia	P. Leccia	Corte	Venaco	Vivario	Vizzavona	Ajaccio
07.45	08.45	09.00	09.10	09.30	09.50	10.45

b) 🚂 service Ajaccio—Bastia, operated by Chemins de Fer de la Corse (ℂ numbers/web site in panel on page 125). Connections from Calvi and l'Ile-Rousse at Ponte Leccia. Following are some convenient times; there are other departures; *collect an up-to-date timetable on arrival!*

Outbound

Ajaccio	Vizzavona	Vivario	Venaco	Corte	P. Leccia	Bastia
09.05	10.15	10.32	10.50	11.09	12.02	13.11

Bastia	P. Leccia	Corte	Venaco	Vivario	Vizzavona	Ajaccio
09.05	10.13	11.07	11.26	11.45	12.04	13.11

Return

Ajaccio	Vizzavona	Vivario	Venaco	Corte	P. Leccia	Bastia
16.44	17.59	18.17	18.36	18.55	19.49	20.52

Bastia	P. Leccia	Corte	Venaco	Vivario	Vizzavona	Ajaccio
14.05	15.13	16.07	16.25	16.44	17.03	18.08

Walk 6: 🚂 as 5 (b) above: Poggio-Riventosa is 5min north of Venaco

Walk 7: bus or train to Corte (as Walk 5), then taxi

Walks 8-10: no suitable public transport

Walk 11: a) 🚂 Calvi—l'Ile-Rouse (as Walk 13); **b)** 🚐 Porto—Calvi, (Autocars SAIB, ℂ 04 95 22 41 99). Departures Mon-Sat from 15/5-10/10 from the Porto junction on the D81 and the Port de Plaisance in Calvi. Departs Porto 08.00; arrives Calvi 11.00; departs Calvi 15.30; arrives Porto 18.00. **c)** 🚐 St-Florent—Calvi (Autocars Santini, ℂ 04 95 37 02 98). Departures Mon-Sat from 6/7-15/9. Departs St-Florent 09.00; arrives Calvi 12.00; departs Calvi 16.00; arrives St-Florent 19.00.

Walk 12: no suitable public transport; nearest base is Calvi (Walk 11)

Walk 13: 🚂 Calvi—l'Ile-Rouse, operated by CFC (as Walk 5 (b) above). Daily 'train-tram' coastal service between Calvi and Ile-Rousse, stopping at all resorts en route. Frequent service in high summer; in shoulder season, typical departures from Calvi are: 09.00, 10.56, 14.16, 17.08; from l'Ile-Rousse at 09.58, 13.20, 15.10, 18.02.

As we mention on page 5, we've been visiting Corsica for many years, first just enjoying the walks in Noel's *Landscapes of Corsica* and, more recently, updating that book. Spending so much time on the island would be prohibitively expensive in hotels, so we go self-catering, but usually have a restaurant meal once a day.

About ten years ago John was diagnosed coeliac and, more recently, lactose intolerant. Food intolerances are becoming ever more common, and we know *there are a lot of you out there!* Even if you have learned to cope at home, it can be very daunting to go on holiday. *Will the food in restaurants be safe? Will I be able to buy gluten- and dairy-free foods?*

If you suffer from food intolerance you have probably already learned at home that what initially seems a penance in fact becomes a challenge and eventually a joy. We eat far healthier meals now than we did before, with fewer additives. Nowhere is this more enjoyable than around the Mediterranean and on Corsica, where olive oil, fish, tomatoes and 'alternative' grains and flours are basic to the diet. Many, many dishes are *naturally* gluten- and dairy-free.

Of course food intolerances *are* restrictive — in the sense that we have to carry, buy or bake gluten-free breads and sweets, and we always need access to dairy-free 'milk', 'cream', 'yoghurt' and 'butter'. So over the years we've sussed out eating gf, df on Corsica, and it's *so simple.*

EAT GF, DF

First edition © 2006
Published by Sunflower Books
PO Box 36061, London SW7 3WS
www.sunflowerbooks.co.uk

ISBN 1-85691-295-7

Cover photograph: Calvi's citadel

Photographs: John Underwood and Noel Rochford
Maps: John Underwood, adapted from French IGN maps (1:25,000)
Series design: Jocelyn Lucas
Cookery editor: Marina Bayliss
A CIP catalogue record for this book is available from the British Library.
Printed and bound in Spain by Grafo Industrias Gráficas, Basauri

Before you go ...
log on to
www.sunflowerbooks.co.uk
and click on '**updates**', to see if we have been notified of any changes to
the routes or restaurants.
When you return ...
do let us know if any routes have changed because of road-building, storm
damage or the like. Have any of our restaurants closed — or any new ones
opened *on the route of the walk?* (Not restaurants in the large towns, please;
these books are not intended to be complete restaurant guides!)
Send your comments to mail@sunflowerbooks.co.uk